THE LITERATURE OF DEATH AND DYING

This is a volume in the Arno Press collection

THE LITERATURE OF DEATH AND DYING

See last pages of this volume for a complete list of titles

THEORY OF SUICIDE

MAURICE L. FARBER

NYT

ARNO PRESS

A New York Times Company

New York / 1977

Reprint Edition 1977 by Arno Press Inc.

Reprinted by permission of
Thomas Y. Crowell Co., Inc.

THE LITERATURE OF DEATH AND DYING
ISBN for complete set: 0-405-09550-3
See last pages of this volume for titles.

Manufactured in the United States of America

Library of Congress Cataloging in Publication Data

Farber, Maurice L 1912-
Theory of suicide.

(The Literature of death and dying)
Reprint of the ed. published by Funk & Wagnalls, New York.
1. Suicide. I. Title. II. Series.
[HV6545.F34 1977] 616.8'5844 76-19568
ISBN 0-405-09564-3

10

Theory of Suicide

FUNK & WAGNALLS New York

MAURICE L. FARBER

THEORY OF SUICIDE

LIBRARY OF CONGRESS CATALOG CARD NUMBER: 68-29778
PUBLISHED BY FUNK & WAGNALLS, *A Division of* READER'S
DIGEST BOOKS, INC.

PRINTED IN THE UNITED STATES OF AMERICA

To My Parents, Harry and Ethel Farber

Foreword

I attempt in this book to develop a general theory of suicide. This entails a theory that isolates those essential variables that are tightly linked to suicide in all cultures and throughout history. I have myself at times doubted, on theoretical grounds, that such a theory is possible. It remains to be seen whether the present attempt is successful. If it is, it appears to provide a type of model not only for many problems in the relation of psychopathology to society but also for broader problems of human social behavior.

This theory is based in part upon my researches in Norway and Denmark, and in the course of the book I make a number of statements about the Norwegian and Danish cultures and modal personalities. These assertions are based upon objective studies. The very human weaknesses to which I occasionally point in both nations, particularly Denmark, are noted with the aim of understanding, diagnosis, and cure. It would seem to be unnecessary to have to point this out, yet recently at a scientific meeting to which I presented some of these findings a young Danish psychiatrist rushed to the microphone when I had finished and delivered a heated attack on my application of "false stereotypes" to his country. Surely this book must be evaluated as good or bad science; the tawdry banners of nationalism should have no place here. I have, I might add, considerable admiration and affection for the people of both countries.

This is not meant to be an exhaustive book about suicide. Much material not relevant to the development of the theory has been omitted and can be found elsewhere. I have also avoided much of the usual paraphernalia of academic writing: the use of footnotes and of bibliographical references linked to every assertion. I have tried also to avoid unnecessarily technical language and jargon. However, it must be recognized that theory construction requires the use of concepts that are clearly and uniquely defined. Here everyday language often will not do; we do not cavil at the physicist for speaking of "mesons" rather than of "teeny-weeny particles." Nonetheless, by limiting technical language and other academic practices as much as possible I hope both to speed the expository flow and to render more visible the building of the theory, permitting easy communication not only with specialists but with a wider circle of interested readers.

Maurice L. Farber

Department of Psychology
University of Connecticut
Storrs, Connecticut

Acknowledgments

Many individuals and institutions have been helpful to me in my work. I would especially like to mention the National Institute of Mental Health, which granted me a fellowship that made possible my research in Scandinavia, and Dr. Erik Rinde, Director of the Institute for Social Research in Norway, who granted me the hospitality and stimulation of his Institute during my stay. Financial assistance for the analysis of my data was provided by the University of Connecticut Research Foundation.

In Copenhagen, Dr. Carl Clemmesen kindly granted me permission to interview suicidal patients at Bispebjerg Hospital. In Oslo, at Ullevål Hospital, such facilities were graciously made accessible by Dr. Herluf Thomstad, Chief of the Psychiatric Division for Women, Dr. Einar Blegen, Chief of the 7th Medical Division, Dr. Anton Jervell, Chief of the 8th Medical Division, and Dr. Kurt Aas, Chief of the 9th Medical Division.

At the Universities of Oslo, Bergen, and Copenhagen, several faculty members made available their classes to me for psychological testing.

Mrs. Sylvia Backer, Dr. Dorothea Braginsky, and Mrs. Anni Von der Lippe provided indispensable research assistance, and Gori Gunwald performed a number of important services.

Mrs. Ellen Blix of the Central Bureau of Statistics in Norway and Miss Karen Dreyer of the statistical department of the National Health Service in Denmark both provided extensive statistical material on suicide.

I had stimulating and instructive discussions with a large number of experts in various fields in both Norway and Denmark on both theoretical and practical levels. Especially helpful were Dr. Erik Schiødt, the Danish suicide expert, Dr. Per Sundby of Ullevål Hospital in Oslo, Dr. Ørnulv Ødegård of Gaustad Hospital in Oslo, Dr. Grethe Paerregaard, who also carried out research on suicide in Denmark, Prof. Villars Lunn of the Rigshospitalet in Copenhagen, and Dr. Bodil Farup, the Danish child psychologist.

Also generous in their help were, in Norway, Finn Carling, Docent Nils Christie, Erik Grönseth, Prof. Sverre Lysgaard, Prof. Ragnar Rommetveit, Prof. Harald Schjelderup, and Docent Åse Gruda Skard.

In Denmark, I conferred with Dr. Gudrun Brun, Dr. Emelie Faber, Dr. Henning Friis, Prof. Franz From, Mr. Fradley Garner, Mr. Erich Goldschmidt, Dr. Henrik Hoffmeyer, Dr. Hedwig Jacoby, Prof. Preben Plum, Prof. E. Tranckjaer Rasmussen, Miss Grethe Schiøler, Dr. Georg K. Stürup, and Prof. Kaare Svalastoga.

In the United States I had useful discussions with Dr. Claus Bahnson and with Dr. Arne Welhaven.

The reader acquainted with the work of Kurt Lewin, my former teacher, will recognize my great intellectual debt to his theoretical system and mode of thought. So, too, have I found of great value the work of some members of the psychoanalytic school.

Finally, I am grateful to my wife, Ruth, for warm encouragement, valuable suggestions, professional editorial assistance, and indispensable services too numerous to list.

I am writing these acknowledgments a number of years after the event and may by now have neglected to note the help of a number of people. If I have, I hope they will understand and forgive me.

O

Contents

Theory of Suicide

1

The Analysis of Suicide

At the very first contemplation of the problem of suicide we encounter curious puzzles and paradoxes. In suicide man uses his power and intelligence to destroy that power and intelligence. His brain is shattered as it still reverberates with the suicidal intention the brain itself initiated. Why does man induce so fearful a thing as death when nothing so terrifying as death is imminent? Why should man act in a way that flies full in the face of his powerful drives toward preservation of the self and of the species?

Our perception of suicide is colored by a strange mixture of revulsion and fascination. Partly this may stem from some awareness of the disturbing paradoxes. Partly, too, it may stir deep-lying self-destructive impulses in many of us. As a consequence, there is often intense emotional overreaction to the concept and even some resistance to scientific research on the problem.

Yet the study of suicide would hardly appear to require a defense. Suicide is an action that takes place in sadness and desperation. It inflicts grief and remorse upon survivors. It deprives us of valuable members of society. It ranks high among the killers of man and is in fact one of the most frequent killers of young adults. Suicide, indeed, kills more frequently than many diseases that are subjected to extensive research.

Viewed as pure behavioral science, the study of suicide has yielded rich material, provided by sociologists, anthropologists, psychiatrists, and psychologists. What is intellectually exciting is that, beyond the mass of factual material and low-level empiricism, attempts have been made by men as different as Durkheim and Freud to fashion broader and more powerful concepts as explanatory devices, that is, a movement toward theory building. But the high cliffs of theory are slippery, and Freud's dictum of 1918 that the problem of suicide had not been solved has remained largely true.

One important insight that has emerged is that suicide is but one of many varieties of self-destruction. Suicide, as we define it in practice, involves a conscious, deliberate attempt to take one's life quickly. Among other varieties of self-destruction, we may note that we do not call it suicide if a man drinks himself to death over a ten-year period, nor do we call it suicide if he shortens his life by drug addiction. Similarly, if a man eats himself to death or otherwise hastens his death by neglecting his health, or if he constantly seeks out dangerous situations such as mountain climbing or auto racing and is killed, we do not usually label it suicide.

Some of these devices are fairly conscious, others less so. The accident-prone may believe they are being careful, yet they behave in curiously self-destructive ways. The amount of self-destruction (and homicide) that occurs through the use of the automobile, almost always recorded as an "accident," is probably enormous, yet peculiarly resistant to observation and analysis.

It is not apt to be considered suicide if an affronted African savage wanders off in the bush or desert and perishes, as is reported to occur. And there is, too, that mysterious phenomenon, of which some apparently authentic cases have been reported, of "psychosomatic death," in which a healthy person dies fairly suddenly of emotional causes.

The wide distribution of self-destructive motives means that they can be studied much more broadly than in suicide alone, or, put differently, that we can learn much about suicide by studying instances that are not strictly suicidal. Moreover, since *depression* is frequently a prelude to suicide, much can be learned about suicide from a study of depression. The point is that the concept of suicide is not an isolated one; it has ramifications reaching deep into the body of psychological knowledge.

There is yet another way in which suicide is not an isolated manifestation: It has roots in the culture in which it occurs. Different suicide rates in different cultures are not haphazard. Rather they reflect suicide-producing forces in the culture which will be manifested in a number of different facets of the culture. In a culture with a high suicide rate we might expect also a high number of unsuccessful suicide attempts, perhaps more depression, and, even in normal people, some susceptibility to depression in the character structure. The culture may produce a high proportion of personalities susceptible to suicide. It may present unusual difficulties in the business of living. In short, suicide rates are an expression of the cultures in which they occur.

Much of the evidence in this book will be congruent with such a psychocultural hypothesis. At this point one might merely note the significant fact that suicide rates for various countries tend to be fairly stable relative to each other over the years. To be sure, the rates change with large social changes, such as wars and economic depressions, and a country may change over a long period from, say, a low-suicide to a high-suicide country; but in the main it is possible to talk of "low" and "high" suicide countries. This fact alone would suggest that there is something characteristic in the culture that produces a certain rate.

By tracing and disentangling the psychological and cultural roots of suicide and by the development of concepts that best describe and subsume them, it now appears possible to move toward a more general theory of suicide. This possibility has recently been denied by a number of suicide experts, but it must be kept in mind that in the history of science any problem has appeared to be in diffuse disarray until the model and concepts have been discovered that bring order to it all. Such an attempt will have to reach across disciplines: academic psychology, psychoanalytic theory, anthropology, and sociology.

Toward the goal of formulating a general theory, an original investigation was carried out in Norway and Denmark; the findings were synthesized with existing knowledge and the whole problem was re-conceptualized. Details of this research are given in Appendix 1.

The original research is based upon the epidemiological fact that Denmark has a very high suicide rate whereas Norway has a low rate (approximately 20 per 100,000 versus 7 per 100,000). This provides an advantageous research design since both countries belong to the same broad culture area, thus narrowing the number of independent variables that might be responsible for the sharply contrasting suicide rates. A strictly experimental method is rarely applicable in the social sciences; it seems probable that the present method comprises one of the practicable analogues in the social sciences to a manipulatory experimental method.

Another cogent reason for selecting these countries is that their suicide statistics are among the most accurate in the world, thus assuring that the contrast is a true one. Even in these countries it is probable that occasional cases escape the official statistics, but this loss is minimal when compared with that in many other countries.

The conclusions that emerge, then, combine the findings of this original work with the considerable body of research and theory that exists into a "best fit," a system of formulations that appears to have optimal explanatory power for the problem of suicide.

At the very outset of the study of suicide, we seem to encounter a curious methodological paradox: As soon as a subject enters the category in which we are interested, that is, he commits suicide, he instantly becomes unavailable because he is dead. Actually, of course, the dilemma is far from hopeless. We can, for instance, uncover much that is relevant about a person after he is dead. Sometimes he has left diaries; sometimes he has received psychotherapy and a great deal is known about him. Friends and intimates can reveal much. Moreover, we can study those who attempted suicide but have survived.

There has been, however, some question among researchers as to whether one may validly draw conclusions about suicide from the study of survivors—the suicide attempters. Stengel, the British investigator, for example, has stressed that they constitute a quite separate category. It might be well to examine this problem, which is but one facet of the basic methodological problem of research on suicide.

Suicide is defined in terms of two basic characteristics: *intention* and *outcome*. To be classed as a suicide, a person must intend to kill himself, and he must actually do so. Intention, however, is not always easily ascertainable. Some cases are quite clear: A jump from the roof of a skyscraper or a bullet through the brain may be accepted as a sign of lethal intention. The taking of a few extra sleeping pills followed immediately by a telephone call to friends informing them of the act or a superficial cutting of the wrists by a wife as she hears her husband's car pulling into the driveway are fairly clear cases of a lack of lethal intention.

But in many cases the intention is not clear. The nature of the method employed is often inconclusive. We cannot always be sure, for example, what an overdose of sleeping pills (a frequent method) signifies in intention. The other possible source of information, asking the subject, is often unrevealing. The survivor is often himself unsure or expresses himself ambiguously.

Between the extremes of a definite lethal intention and a definite intention to go on living at least two other intentions emerge. One has been called "the gamble with death." Here the subject's intention is to die or not to die, contingent upon outside forces over which he has no control, and he arranges such a situation. Playing "Russian roulette" is but one rather rare example. A rejected mistress may take an overdose of a sedative when her lover may or may not come to see her. If he comes, he saves her and she lives; if not, she dies. It will be seen that there is a rather neat testing of the environment here, with the outcome determined by the results of the test: "If he loves me enough to come tonight, I want to live, and I will; if he does not love me, has abandoned me, and does not come tonight, I want to die, and I will."

It is of interest that this kind of suicidal act can be institutionalized in a society. Raymond Firth, the British anthropologist, describes such a practice in Tikopia. The insulted man seizes a canoe and paddles out into the great reaches of the Pacific. When his absence is noted, a search party paddles out to find him. If they do, he will go on living. Again, there is the test: "If they care for me enough, they will come and find me; if they don't, I want to die."

A somewhat more ambiguous intention may be called "getting away." Often in my interviews the patient would say, in reply to a question about his intentions, something like: "I don't know. I just couldn't stand things any longer. I just had to get away from it all." He did not necessarily wish to die, but he did want to black out of his consciousness, at least for a time, his sadness and desperation.

Outcomes are clearer than intentions: The subject survives or he dies. But we cannot infer intention from outcome; outcome is determined by a number of contingencies.

The methodological problem of the kinds of cases available can be clarified by the construction of a simple formal model which cross-tabulates intention and outcome, using only the clear-cut extremes of intention.

		OUTCOME	
		Death	Survival
INTENTION	To die	A	B
	Not to die	C	D

The cases in Cell A, which meet both definitional criteria of suicide, are the only "true" suicides. They are not, obviously, available for direct study after the event. This group contains more males than females and more old people than young.

The cases in Cell B are particularly interesting, because in intention, that is, psychologically, they are similar to the Cell A or "true" suicides. Such cases certainly occur: The subject overestimates the lethal effects of the dosage; he is surprised during the attempt; he is unexpectedly rescued. Since these cases survive, they are apt to be grouped indiscriminately with the Cell D cases. When clearly identified, however, they are instances that have cracked the methodological dilemma and can be studied as "true" suicides.

There is a bitter irony in the situation of the Cell C cases. They did not intend to die, yet they do. The lethal effects of a drug are underestimated; a husband comes home later than he is expected. These cases are not usually distinguished from the Cell A cases despite their rather considerable motivational differences.

Probably the largest group of cases falls into Cell D. These are the "true" attempters, the perpetrators of the suicidal gesture, the criers for help, as Farberow and Shneidman have called them. There are more young people than old in this group, and more females than males. It is the kind of case a researcher working directly with suicide is most apt to find available.

Something of value can be learned from the study of cases in each of the cells, but it is important to know in which cell they belong. It should be noted that a number of Cell D cases eventually move into Cell A; that is, attempters may well later become achievers. The fact that on average attempters differ from achievers in age and sex does not mean that we must exclude attempters from the study of suicide. They have selected self-destructive methods, even if not yet lethal ones. Their self-destructive motives are not as intense as in completed suicides and their motivational pattern is somewhat different, but there is much that is similar between the two. To conclude, as some investigators have, that these are "different populations"—with the implication that one cannot learn anything about suicide from the study of attempters—is not justified. One can learn much about a disease from a study of mild cases of it.

The Basic Paradigm

In the broadest theoretical terms, what manner of act is suicide? What initial conceptual framework can be erected within which we may place the more detailed and specific relevant variables? It would seem that the following expression provides such a general framework:

$$S = f\,(V, D)$$

which states that S, the probability of an individual's committing suicide, is a function of V, his vulnerability, and D, the degree of certain deprivations. The expression may be read on a sociological level as stating that *the frequency of suicide in a population is a function of the frequency of individuals possessing a certain vulnerability in that population and the extent of certain deprivations in that population.*

This model of a two-factor interaction is essential as a starting point. Theories that stress exclusively the one factor or the other must founder. Earlier psychoanalytic theories tended to focus upon the nature of the vulnerability, whereas sociological theories have tended to stress exclusively different forms of deprivation. The great early theoretician of suicide Emile Durkheim failed, as we shall see, mainly because he was largely blind to the vulnerability component.

It is useful and enlightening to examine limiting cases of each component. A manic-depressive psychotic in a deep depression may commit suicide, although little is occurring in the outside world that we might call a deprivation. The depression and guilt are overwhelmingly generated from within: The V term in the equation is large, the D term very small.

In contrast a psychologically healthy person, faced with the certainty of being tortured to death, might commit suicide. Here the V term is very small, the D term overwhelming.

Most cases of suicide fall, of course, between these two limiting cases. *Suicides in the main are committed by psychologically damaged personalities confronted by a deprivational situation.* It is the nature of the vulnerability, the kind of deprivations, and their interactions that must be analyzed.

2

A Disease of Hope

Of all the possible concepts that have been or might be related to suicide, which is the most closely, the most powerfully related? Hope in its full scale—ranging from the most buoyant optimism down to the blackest despair—is, I believe, that concept.

What, then, is hope? It entails confident expectation that a desired outcome will occur. The objects of hope and its level of intensity represent central determinants of human behavior. For man is a future-oriented animal, perhaps uniquely so. Much of his world is one of expectations. The object of hope may be narrow, as when one is hopeful of being served a good dinner, or the object may be one's whole life outlook, as in facing a debacle in one's career. It is with this broad focus of hope that we are primarily concerned. *It is when the life outlook is of despairing hopelessness that suicide* occurs.

Folk wisdom has long been aware of the central importance of hope. Proverbs and expressions, worn so smooth that their bite is lost, express this: "Hope springs eternal in the human breast" (Pope), "Where there is life there is hope" (Cicero, Cervantes), and "grasping at straws." Each expresses something insightful about the dynamics of hope.

It is curious that hope as a psychological concept has been but meagerly recognized and explored. In traditional psychoanalytic thought the emphasis has mainly been upon unconscious processes to the neglect, until recently, of external social events and of such ego functions as the maintenance of hope. In current academic psychology, where the most irrelevant concept psychologically is often judged to be the most scientific, many would not for a moment consider the use of a concept that is patently so central and is even present in everyday speech.

Some recognition of hope as a concept has, of course, taken place. Kurt Lewin described it and placed it in his formal psychological system, specifically in the future time-perspective, the future outlook as it exists at present. He did little exploration, however, of its empirical relationships, dealing mainly with small emotions in level-of-aspiration experiments.

Many years ago, as a student of Lewin's, I carried out research that demonstrated that the degree of suffering of prisoners in a penitentiary was related to their hopes (inversely) and to the structure of their future outlook. In a later study I showed that an individual's preferences among the days of the week are determined less by the activities usually carried out on that day than by his hopes on that day.

More recently, Erik Erikson performed the important feat of inserting the concept of hope into the framework of a modified psychoanalytic theory, by conceiving of it as the positive and healthful side of the oral phase of psychosexual development. As a consequence, it becomes potentially possible to link hope with developmental stages, with trust and mistrust, with child rearing, with psychosis, and with other important areas.

A recent book on suicide, Kobler and Stotland's *The End of Hope*, promises in its title a serious and analytic treatment of hope as a concept, but in fact treats it only in a generally descriptive fashion.

One might note in a speculative vein that it is quite possible that hope has deep biological roots and that a primitive unverbalized kind of hope operates in animals. When this "hope" is severely reduced, the animal may act to hasten death. Many animals are reported to "crawl away to die." The domestic cat, for example, when mortally ill, often leaves the protection and care of its owner's house and goes off to die. This might be interpreted as a kind of instinctive "suicide." It is possible that vestiges of such an instinctive tendency are present in man, that when continued life is felt to be hopeless, death is more quickly embraced. Such behavior, especially when it entails self-removal from the group and isolation of a disease bearer, would clearly have survival value for the species. In any case, it is doubtful that such tendencies in man, if they exist, could suffice to explain human suicide. The possibility that animals below man have a tendency to end life under hopeless conditions suggests, however, that deep and overlaid in man some fragmentary instinctual suicidal tendencies may exist.

Hope is not an ultimate particle of psychology. It is in itself an outcome of the interaction of two factors, one in the personality and the other in the situation. Individuals differ from each other in their ability to sustain hope in the face of a given difficulty: One rejected lover commits suicide; another before very long looks in his address book and telephones another girl. There is also the story of the drunk who comes to a telegraph pole, proceeds to feel his way carefully all around it, and announces tragically: "It's hopeless. I'm hemmed in."

The personality factor might best be called *the sense of competence*, as suggested by Robert W. White, a basic pervasive feeling in the individual that he has the resources within himself to cope with the demands of living. The foundations of this sense of competence, as we shall see in more detail later, are probably laid down quite early in life. It will be quickly noted that this concept bears some similarities to older concepts in psychology. Alfred Adler's "feelings of inferiority" might be seen as representing a low sense of competence, but the use to which Adler put his concept is rather different from the construction that I shall attempt here. The concept is related also to Erik Erikson's theories of psychosexual development, particularly to the trust-mistrust polarity of the oral phase and to later developments like the sense of mastery. The most recent isolation, refinement, and appreciation of the concept has been achieved by Robert W. White. The concept is used here very much in the sense that White has developed it. As used here, we are concerned with *the basic sense of efficacy in mastering one's environment*, a broad underlying feeling that has both conscious and unconscious components and colors much of our behavior. *This basic sense of competence and its disruption are central in suicide and possibly in mental disorders in general.*

The situational factor that contributes to hope in interaction with the sense of competence is the degree of threat leveled against the individual's being able to sustain a minimally acceptable existence. The loss of or abandonment by a loved one, the loss of one's fortune and position, the ravages of a disease—these are the kinds of threats that place in jeopardy the ability to maintain a minimally acceptable existence.

More formally, then,

$$H = f\left(\frac{C}{T}\right)$$

in which C is the Sense of Competence and T the level of Threat to acceptable life conditions.

C, the Sense of Competence, is to a considerable extent subjective but is amenable to assessment by clinical interview and tests. It cannot be simply and directly reported by a subject, since it contains unconscious elements. Nonetheless, one may be reasonably confident that reliable estimates can be made.

T, the Threat to acceptable life conditions, is better conceptualized as an objective variable rather than a phenomenological one. Although individuals doubtless differ as to what they perceive to be a threat, this perception derives partly from the Sense of Competence. To use the *perceived* threat as the T variable would cause overlapping of T and C, since what one sees as threatening is partly determined by C. The solution is to define T in terms of a social-psychological scale of threats for a given culture, thus keeping C and T independent of each other.

The initial crude formula can now be somewhat refined: It was pointed out that, broadly, suicide was a function of a vulnerability in the personality and a deprivation. The vulnerability can now be asserted to be a low Sense of Competence and the deprivation better described as a Threat to acceptable life conditions. Thus:

$$S = f\left(\frac{1}{\text{Hope}}\right) = f\left(\frac{T}{C}\right)$$

that is, the probability of Suicide varies inversely with the level of Hope and also directly with a Threat to acceptable life conditions and inversely with the level of the Sense of Competence.

The sense-of-competence component in hope is found to be omnipresent when suicides are analyzed. The extreme limiting instance is found in psychotic depressives, whose sense of competence has sunk so low that even everyday life is too great a threat for them to tolerate. But relatively normal persons too can feel at times that their resources are insufficient to cope with the threat.

The case of Ernest Hemingway reveals this most vividly. Hemingway had always been proud of his competence, quelling any doubts he may have had by his work, by his lovemaking, and by those ultramasculine activities: boxing, going to war, deep-sea fishing. Now he was old, sick, depressed—none of these available to him. His conversations toward the end reveal the tremendous diminution in his sense of competence, and thus, his hope. Indeed, material revealed in his autobiographical writings and in biographical material suggests that there was always a certain fragility in his sense of competence.

Suicide in old age, when it is not precipitated by economic misery or acute illness, often reveals clearly the role of the sense of competence. The aged observe their powers failing and hope dims. The mother of a Danish friend, a matriarch of apparently strong character, committed suicide without having any acute difficulties but suffering only from a decline in her formidable powers.

The threat component possesses what might be called a topographical dimension that is peculiarly relevant to suicide. This is what has been called the "space of free movement" by Kurt Lewin. It refers to the areas of life open to an individual, the activities and positions into which he is free to move. Normally, a person has available to him at any given time a number of acceptable courses of action from among which he may choose. In the psychological situation of suicide the interaction of a low sense of competence and external threat results in a highly constricted space of free movement.

This is equivalent, of course, to a low level of hope. To a person in this situation there seems to be no course of action; there is no one to whom he can turn who will extricate him from a hopeless situation in which the conditions of life threaten to become intolerable. This is most clearly seen in the suicide of the cornered gangster, his hideaway surrounded by many police, shooting it out with the police. He has already killed one policeman, and a number of other charges hang over his head. As the police close in, as his space of free movement narrows to hopelessness, he turns his gun upon himself.

Here the "no exit" character of suicide is most clearly seen; self-induced death is the only exit. But it is true also in other situations that "close in." The suicide of the Swedish financial manipulator Ivar Kreuger, which shook the financial world, followed the threatened exposure of his fraud and swindles, so colossal that there was now no tolerable way out. Nor is there in the case of the suicide of an old man suffering from a painful and incurable illness. *Suicide occurs when there appears to be no available path that will lead to a tolerable existence.*

The evidence that it is hope (with its components) that is the variable most powerfully and proximally related to suicide is exceedingly strong. The clinical evidence appears in the work of many students of suicide, although the concept may not be labeled as hope nor its full theoretical implications developed. In our intensive interviews with those who had attempted suicide the centrality of hope and its destruction in case after case was impressive.

Many suicide notes reveal the loss of hope and the unacceptability of the future outlook. For example, Harriet Westbrook Shelley wrote, after being abandoned by her poet husband:

Too wretched to exert myself, lowered in the opinion of everyone, why should I drag out a miserable existence? embittered by past recollections and no one ray of hope to rest on for the future.

Our questionnaire findings with normal Norwegian and Danish students also support this analysis, at least indirectly. (It will be recalled that Danes tend to commit suicide more frequently than Norwegians.) Danes, we found, tend to view life less hopefully than Norwegians. For example, there is also some support for the assertion that Danes have a more restricted psychological space of free movement:

Item: What possibilities that are both practical and hopeful are open to a person who finds his or her life situation highly unsatisfactory?

Percentage replying "There is nothing he can do":

Danes:	5.0
Norwegians:	.6

(This difference and all differences reported hereafter are statistically significant at beyond the 5% level.)

Furthermore, it was found that Danes do not engage in as much "deferred gratification"—the willingness to put off current satisfaction for future ends—as the Norwegians. Deferred gratifications involve the sustaining of long-range hopes and thus suggest again a greater Norwegian hopefulness.

Item: I do without many things in the present because of my plans for my future career.

Percentage agreeing:

Danes:	35.3
Norwegians:	52.3

Several other items reveal that the Norwegians are more future oriented. For example:

Item: I live mostly in the present and let the future take care of itself.

Percentage agreeing:

Danes:	37.5
Norwegians:	24.7

A hopeful future orientation is antisuicidal; a focus on the present may represent a despairing feeling that the future will not bring anything desirable.

The greater fragility of hope among the Danes in contrast with the Norwegians is shown in the greater tendency of the Danes to become depressed, as revealed in our data:

Item: Fairly often I feel sad and depressed.

The percentage feeling that the statement applies very strongly to themselves:

Norwegians:	12.9
Danes:	21.0

Something of the weaker sense of competence in the Danes is suggested, I believe, in their feelings about the influence of their country in world affairs. (Denmark, it will be noted, actually has a larger population than Norway.)

Item: My country has considerable influence in world affairs.

The percentage disagreeing strongly with the statement:

Norwegians:	59.5
Danes:	79.0

It is striking, too, in this connection, how often in conversation with Danes that they will point out: "We are a small country."

Further, one of the most salient observations made in my analysis of Danish cartoons was that the typical Dane in them is almost invariably a *little* man of childlike proportions. The self-image of the Dane appears to lack the adult sense of competence.

There is a characteristic Norwegian behavior called "skippertak," which involves the procrastination of a task until the last moment and then the storming of it in a great burst of energy. This may reveal, among other things, a relatively strong sense of competence —the feeling that one has the resources in the final "battle" to conquer the task.

Yet other indications of low hope exist in the Danish culture.

For example, our content analysis of the beloved fairy tales of Hans Christian Andersen reveals that beneath their charm runs a strain of pessimism. The toad may have a jewel in its head, but when it ventures forth into the world it loses its life.

Sometimes nature or politics acts upon man in the mass in a manner that has something of the logical design of an experiment, so that conclusions can be drawn from it. Such was the case when the Berlin wall divided East from West Berlin in 1961. Before the border was closed on August 13, the suicide rate in East Berlin was about one a day. Within a few days after the closing of the border, the suicide rate in East Berlin rose to about twenty-five a day. Perhaps half of these were "border crossers," that is, East Berliners who had worked in West Berlin before August 13.

This increase in suicide seems clearly to have been a matter of the withdrawal of hope. As one East Berliner put it at the time: "Millions of people have never thought of escape simply because they knew they could always get away if they had to. I could kick myself for being so stupid. August 13 was not like June 17, 1953, when the East German workers rose against the Russian troops. In fact, the contrast was shocking. Eight years ago our people threw stones at the Soviet tanks. We were intoxicated with the hope of freedom. This time we were bewildered and terrified. There is no hope in East Berlin today, only fear and utter resignation." The relationship between hope and suicide is here eloquently demonstrated.

Another line of evidence comes from the behavior of Jews faced with being sent to Nazi concentration camps. For the last few years before 1940 the average number of suicides in Holland for the month of May was 71.2. In May, 1940, immediately after the Nazi take-over, there were 371. It was in *anticipation* of the horror of the camps that the wave of suicides took place. In the camps themselves, in the very presence of death, there were few suicides as long as a shred of hope remained. As soon as it became clear that there was indeed no hope, a second wave of suicides took place. Similarly, in the year 1190 in York, England, some 500 Jews were reported to have committed suicide to avoid religious persecution.

The suicide of the ardent, rejected lover is based upon his having embraced the delusion that he literally cannot live without his beloved, that without her life is hopeless. This is apt to occur, of course, in those in whom the sense-of-competence component of hope is low and sustainable only in a dependent relationship.

The relation between age and suicide gathers illumination from an analysis in terms of hope. It has long been known that, in the main in most Western countries, the frequency of suicide increases with age. Below the age of 15, suicides are extremely rare, with the curve rising in the United States from 3.6 per 100,000 in the 15–19-year group, to one of 27.9 per 100,000 in the 75–84-year group.

It is highly probable that this curve coincides with the curve of hopelessness with age. The young are intrinsically so buoyantly hopeful about their lives that they need not intellectualize about it. For the young adult with an infinity of years lying ahead, failures and losses can be shaken off; he still has strength, energy, and time. By middle age early hopes may still be unrealized and now be perceived as unrealizable; chronic illnesses may have developed and it becomes clear that one does not have many years to live. Patently, the general level of hope about one's life is markedly lower. By old age these tragedies may be sharper, with more illness, loss of feeling of competence, and more poignant hopelessness. The curves of age against suicide rate and age against hopelessness in a given culture are in all probability pretty much identical.

Yet it should be clear that the relationship between age and suicide is neither direct nor fixed. A great deal depends upon the role assigned and accruing to the stages of life in a particular society and the hope generated by the roles. If old age is heaped with comfort and honor, the rate for the old may not be extremely high. In accordance with our theory, any period of life could be a high-suicide period if hope and its components are severely damaged.

A striking illustration can be found in Japan, where the suicide rate for youths is extraordinarily high. Suicide is the most frequent cause of death for people under thirty, with the rate for men of this age group reaching the shocking figure of 80 per 100,000. A major situational cause would appear to lie in the school examination system. The advanced school examination is crucial. If one passes, one is assured a good job and an advantageous marriage. Failure means an inferior career, low status throughout the rest of one's life, a destruction of hope. It is among these failures and anticipators of failure that the suicide rate is so distressingly high. The condition of youth itself, if it is deprived of hope, need not insulate against suicide.

In contemporary Japan old age appears to present yet another point in the life cycle during which hope is threatened, and the suicide rate for this group is unusually high. Two economic factors are involved here: the necessity for old people on farms to continue working because of the exodus of the young to the cities, and second the gap between the age of retirement and the age of eligibility for government pensions which results in considerable economic misery during the interim period. Clearly, although there are a number of potential destroyers of hope that are almost inevitable in old age, the culture will determine whether their impact is gentle or severe.

Although suicides are infrequent among the young, suicide attempts are not. These attempts often represent a "cry for help," or desperate maneuvers, often successful, for eliciting certain behavior from other people, as Stengel has shown. Clearly there is a residue of vigorous hope in these efforts that stop short of inducing death, an intrinsic hope in youth even in its desperation.

As might be expected, it is among the old that attempts are more serious and much more often successful. They know that in the normal course of events death cannot be far off, that their worn bodies cannot be rejuvenated, their chronic maladies cured, or their lonely lives filled with friends. The methods selected are thus more lethal ones; no undercurrent of hope stays their hand.

Suicidal Migrations

There exists a constant movement of people from places in which they are frustrated and unhappy to places where they *hope* they will find gratification. In the modern world, with transportation and travel easily available, this recourse occurs on a massive scale. A certain proportion of these people, motivated by a high but fragile hope, constitute potential suicides. These movements may justifiable be called "suicidal migrations."

Thus it is that in the United States there is a flow of the personally unhappy, the occupationally dissatisfied, the seekers after love, to California, to Nevada, to Florida, avidly seeking fulfillment. The hopes of many, often the last great hopes of a series of hopes and disappointments, are dashed. Suicides and suicide attempts follow. Thus it is that these states and particularly the glamorous cities in them have suicide rates far higher than the rest of the country. The rate in San Francisco is many times the national average; that of Los Angeles is also strikingly high. Miami is another high-suicide city. The fact that these cities may contain a higher proportion of old people, who, it will be recalled, have high rates, does not fully account for the high rates of these cities, in which many of the suicides are not old. Nor, of course, can it be maintained that all migrants to these places are the desperately hopeful and potentially suicidal; it is simply a matter of greater frequency.

Traditionally, it has been customary to stress the conditions of city life, the greater loneliness, the rootlessness, as the explanation of the higher urban rates. These may well be factors, but the possibility that cities and particular parts of cities are both lodestones and concentration points for certain *psychological* types has been insufficiently developed in the social sciences.

Certain occupations may well play a similar role. For example, a recent study reveals extraordinarily high suicide rates among Swedish sailors. The conditions of the sailor's life may play some part, but a major factor is doubtless the movement into the occupation of certain psychological types, vulnerable in their ability to sustain hope, and, therefore, under certain stressful conditions, suicide-prone.

The use of the concept of hope may well throw light upon a number of persistent problems in the theory of suicide. For example, it has long been noted that suicide rates drop during times of war. A number of explanations have been offered, usually in terms of the expression of aggression, which may be of some validity, but it has rarely been suggested that wars are also times of hope. Despite various possible material hardships, civilian wartime populations are often imbued with great and often irrational hopes for victory and a changed world beyond. In the losing countries the rise in suicides begins *before* the war is over, when the war becomes hopeless.

Another relationship, one that has had a number of tortured explanations, is that between social class and suicide. The data here are somewhat equivocal but seem to point fairly consistently to higher rates in the topmost and lowest social classes. With regard to the lowest classes, the role of hope is easy to perceive. The various hardships of grinding poverty are surely sufficient, for many, to extinguish hope, and the evidence is strong that the removal of these hardships lowers the suicide rate for these disadvantaged groups. With regard to the upper classes, the explanation is less clear and probably more multifaceted. They are doubtless encouraged to set high expectations for themselves. If these expectations are disappointed, their sense of competence and level of hope could be severely lowered. Possibly, too, they are expected to exert more control over aggression, which, as we shall see, constitutes an attack upon the sense of competence and upon hope.

The use of hope as a central concept allows for an ordering of previously disparate material. Depression, for example, that frequent precursor of suicide, can be seen as a state of low hope. A schematic scale of hope can be constructed to which various psychological conditions related to suicide may be ordered, as follows:

	High	Uncontrolled elation with unrealistically high hope, as in manic psychoses.
		Good moods, within normal range.
		Normal, realistic, "healthy" hope.
HOPE		Mild depressions, within normal range.
		Suicidal gesture, without lethal intent.
		The gamble with death.
	Low	{ True suicide, with full lethal intent. / Deep retarded depression. }

Thus both mania and depression, as well as the various kinds of suicide attempts and true suicide, are brought into relation by the use of hope as an organizing concept.

It will be seen that true suicide is placed at a somewhat higher level of hope than is the deep retarded depression. Clinical observation suggests that suicide may not take place at the very nadir of despair but rather at some point in hope a little above that. It has been observed, for example, that often a suicide takes place after a patient has begun to emerge from his deepest depression, when, ironically, his associates have begun to breathe more easily. The deepest depressions often involve a retardation that precludes most activities, including suicide, which require some degree of energy and initiative. It is also quite possible that the making of the tacit decision to commit suicide in itself acts as a source of relief because a way out of the despair has been found, a sort of minor hope. Thus the mood improves after the decision to commit suicide has definitely been made.

These considerations open several possibilities. It may be that the equation stating that the probability of suicide varies inversely with hope does not hold at the lowest levels of hope. Or, better, it is possible that the equation does hold and that the secondary hope engendered by the decision to commit suicide is of a quite different character, not referring to hope about life, and therefore not properly a part of H. This would place the probability of suicide at the lowest levels of the scale, together with deep depression. Another possibility is to define S cognitively as the probability of the *decision* to commit suicide; here it is only the *act* of suicide, not the decision, that would take place at a higher level of hope. In view of these open questions, true suicide, although placed above deep depression in the scheme, is tentatively bracketed together with it.

It must be noted that as a person descends the scale of hope he need not carry out each of the various activities on the scale, such as the suicidal gesture or the gamble with death. He may pass through these levels too rapidly for any crystallization and execution of such ideas to take place; some stabilization at a particular level seems to be a prerequisite for action.

Suicide, then, is in the main an act of hopelessness, of despair and desperation. Some theorists have maintained something of the opposite. A number of psychoanalysts have pointed to the hope of rejoining a lost loved one after death. Hendin, for example, in his *Suicide and Scandinavia,* suggests that in the Danish culture this motive plays an important role. My own studies of the Danes did not support this assertion. In my intensive interviews with Danish suicide attempters, this notion did not emerge as of any importance. Furthermore, only 12.9% of our Danish sample of normal individuals indicated that they believed in the possibility of rejoining loved ones after death. Actually, a considerably higher percentage (27.0%) believed this in low-suicide Norway. Similarly, nation-wide public opinion polls carried out in these countries show a markedly higher proportion of the population believing in life after death in Norway than in Denmark.

It has also been stated, for example by Karl Menninger, that the suicide may represent a hope of returning to the serene bliss of an intra-uterine existence. Again, there appears to be little evidence for this. If it is asserted that these motives are quite unconscious and therefore accessible only to psychoanalysts and not to other investigators, it is still necessary that some firm evidence, even if indirect, be supplied. For the great mass of suicidal cases such has not been forthcoming. On the basis of the hard evidence, suicide is basically a running away from, a bursting out of an unbearable situation rather more than a hopeful embracing of something prospectively attractive. It is better seen as a quick self-induced death chosen in preference to the certain prospect of an unbearable life leading somehow to a nameless horrible death. To be sure, as we have seen, there may be some sweet relief after the decision to commit suicide has been made, in the prospect that the anguish will soon be over, but there are few for whom death is more attractive than life, unless life has proved unbearable.

The probability of suicide is an inverse function of the level of hope. The old adage "Where there is life, there is hope" attests to man's valiant struggles to maintain hope. But we might also say: "Where there is hope, there is life."

3

The Vulnerable

Our initial model asserted that the probability of suicide is a function of the interaction of psychological vulnerability and certain deprivations. Most suicides, that is, possess personality structures that render them vulnerable. We have noted, too, that in some rare instances, the vulnerability may be minimal, the subject relatively healthy psychologically, but the deprivation factor overwhelming, as in the case of a man about to be tortured to death or an old man dying of an incurable and agonizing disease. But these are not the typical suicides. Far more frequently, the suicide is psychologically damaged.

One immediately apparent line of evidence for this is the extraordinarily disturbed life histories of most suicides. In my own investigation, and in that of others who cared to look, there is revealed again and again a series of inadequacies, of failures. Sometimes there is alcoholism, sometimes divorce, sometimes occupational instability, almost always disordered interpersonal relations. Naive theorists have conceived of these failures as merely unfortunate accidents that might occur to anyone and have concluded that the suicide was *nothing but* a consequence of these misfortunes. Actually, a close examination of their failures reveals clearly that in most cases the failure itself is caused mainly by psychological indaquacies in the subjects. These failures, to be sure, now come to be deprivations and threats to which the subject may respond suicidally.

The term "psychologically damaged" should not be interpreted to mean "psychotic" or "mentally ill." The problem of whether suicides are mentally ill has produced disagreement and confusion. In one sense the answer is a matter of definition; if the suicidal act is perceived as a "crazy" piece of behavior, then the subject must be viewed as "crazy"; just as all criminals could be viewed as mentally ill if crimes were viewed as "sick" acts. This kind of thinking is not fruitful, however, and a more rigorous and empirical approach is necessary.

The great majority of suicides are not psychotic, that is, they are not out of touch with reality, they can care for themselves, they are not committable to a mental hospital on the basis of their symptoms. They may be temporarily depressed, distraught, and desperate at the time of the act, but so are at times many normal people who do not commit suicide. To speak of "temporary insanity" may constitute a legal dodge, but it is misleading because psychosis is a more extended process in time and not momentary.

Perhaps as many as one quarter of suicidal cases *are* psychotic, though a precise estimate is hardly possible. Mental hospitals must, of course, exercise close surveillance over certain kinds of patients, particularly depressives, because of the danger of suicide. But most suicides are not in this category. Yet we have labeled them as "psychologically damaged." What is the nature of this damage?

We suggested earlier as an initial broad generalization that suicides possess a low ability to sustain hope, that they are thrown into despair more easily concerning their ability to cope with situations than are the psychologically healthy.

This fragility of the ability to sustain hope, we suggested, is based upon an impaired feeling of competence. This feeling, a deep-seated pervasive sense that may be neither easily verbalized nor even conscious, may color much of a subject's behavior. Basically, such a person *doubts that his powers are sufficient to handle the demands of life.*

Very frequently, the feeling of competence is sensitively connected with the life of another person. The subject feels competent only when succored, protected, led, by a person perceived as strong—a parent, a spouse, a lover—in a relationship that is markedly symbiotic. Thus it is that the disruption of such a relationship, the loss of such a person, is often a potent factor in suicide. The cry, "I cannot live without you," may be, subjectively at least, literally true.

This orientation has been described in psychiatric thought as *dependence.* Erich Fromm speaks of the authoritarian seeking for "the magic helper," and others have developed related concepts. What is important to note is that the concept of dependence is subsumed under the present larger concept of the sense of competence: The dependent person is low in his sense of competence and clings for support to a figure perceived as stronger. The dependent personality is but one kind of personality suffering from a low sense of competence.

I believe it can be demonstrated that a low sense of competence lies beneath a wide range of traditional psychiatric diagnostic categories and can be shown to be basic in their psychodynamics. In different disorders different mechanisms develop to handle various degrees of a low sense of competence, resulting in different symptomatology. The manic, for example, denies that he feels incompetent and depressed by an extreme manifestation of its opposite in elation and self-confidence.

The feeling of abandonment, of helplessness, of incompetence, generates an unassuageable hunger for supplies of love, succorance, goods, which—it is hoped—will provide strength and relief. The demands are in the main made upon people close to the subject—parents, spouses, lovers. These individuals cannot supply what is demanded. Out of this frustration grows a great rage against those who appear to refuse the demands.

For the function of rage is to destroy a frustration or threat and sometimes to beat the frustrator into granting what is demanded.

But the attack cannot take place, because the withholder is also the major giver or, at least, the potential giver. A furious child cannot kill his mother, for then he himself perishes. Some rage may break out; most does not.

Thus we have a person bursting with more or less strangulated rage, unable to leave his symbiotic relationship. His psychological space of free movement is severely limited. The problem is well-nigh insoluble.

The effect of this psychic bind is a further assault upon the feeling of competence. To be unable to use a basic weapon—aggression—that one holds in one's hand, to be unable to solve an anguishing problem, is to undermine yet further the sense of competence.

The rage and its purpose are, to be sure, not acceptable to the subject's values and as a consequence guilt is generated, leading yet more intensely to feelings of low self-esteem, self-hatred, and incompetence. In some cases the guilt reaches a degree of intensity such that the victim feels he must expiate his wickedness by self-punishment. This adds additional energy to the basic self-destructive impulses growing out of the shattered sense of competence. All the influences in this syndrome act synergically in an assault upon the basic sense of competence, leading to a feeling of helplessness in the face of environmental blows and demands and thus to hopelessness.

Hopelessness is often manifested by depression, which is a frequent precursor of the suicide itself. The symptoms of depression, the feeling of incompetence, of helplessness and lack of resources, of no paths open, often of guilt, the repressed rage lurking beneath the sadness, all reflect the processes that have been described.

The case of Ernest Hemingway, touched upon earlier, is revealing. There is good reason to believe that he suffered from a severely injured sense of competence. His mother was almost pathologically domineering, insisting upon absolute obedience in both her husband, who himself committed suicide, and her children. To be dominated means, often, to have one's competence denied by someone apparently well able to judge.

But Hemingway possessed splendid resources: a powerful physique and literary talent. His account of his early days in Paris in *A Moveable Feast* reflect a sunny zest, a *joie de vivre*, a feeling of his powers, joy in his marriage. Yet even then the gnawing doubts beneath began to be disruptive. His need for reassurance concerning his competence led him to be unfaithful to the wife he loved, and to the destruction of his first marriage.

The need to still the basic doubts led to an overcompensatory life style: the passion for boxing, big-game hunting, sport-fishing, bullfighting—all, in a way, advertisements of ultramasculine competence. The role of "Papa" that he cultivated was part of the same defensive system.

Even at the height of his success there were signs of basic difficulties. He was unable to establish a sound marriage, having had four wives in all, which suggests ambivalence, mistrust, and probably basic dependence in relation to women. His tendency to marry successful career women suggests again the basic dependency, the unconscious seeking of a strong woman to succor him from his own deep-felt weakness. Hemingway's friend Hotchner reports that Hemingway complained that his last wife was tough and unsympathetic with his suffering, again a reflection of the ambivalence, the demanding love-hate so characteristic of this kind of character structure.

In his later years his powers began to fail him and their fruits to be withdrawn. This, essentially, was the blow that precipitated the descent to suicide. He had been seriously injured in accidents, his blood pressure was high, he was medically advised against sex, and his literary work had been mercilessly attacked.

The powerful fortress of his defenses began to crumble; he was no longer the great boxer, the great white hunter, the great fisherman, the unquestionably great writer, the great lover. These riches, which up to now had stilled his doubts, were no longer available; and the ghastly hopelessness and despair broke through in depression (what Hemingway called his "Black Ass"), guilt at his aggression, and persecutory delusions. He could no longer write. The last section of *A Moveable Feast*, written as he was breaking down, is depressed and colored by persecutory delusions. That he broke down into psychosis before his suicide suggests the severity of the early damage. His conversations during his mental illness reveal something of his basic lack of a sense of competence.

These are, I believe, the bare bones of the man Ernest Hemingway. If the complexity and many-sidedness of a human life has not been presented, it must be remembered that we are concerned here mainly with the theoretical core of suicide.

Although it is suggested here that depression essentially is a response to a life situation perceived as hopeless, it is a complex manifestation that may have a number of functions. I would suggest that depression may be seen as a way station toward death. But it may also be, as Rado has suggested, a desperate attempt to elicit the love and care that is craved. It is as if the depressed victim is saying: "See what you have done to me. Now you must undo it." These are not contradictory views of depression. We have seen again and again in psychopathology that a symptom embodies a number of functions.

This, then, is the personality structure that might be described as being the "pure case" of the suicide-prone. To be sure, in different cultures the relative weights of the constituents may differ. In some, one will see more clearly the basic despair of helpless abandonment, in some the frustrated rage, in some the guilt at the rage.

Similarly, in individual cases one or another of these processes may be strong or weak. In psychotic suicides the sense of competence may be so low as to have destroyed some mechanisms of defense or to have sharply exaggerated others.

These cultural and individual variations have led many students of suicide either to complex and detailed classifications of the varieties of suicidal personalities or, even further, to conclude that there are too many kinds of suicide to allow for general formulations. I would suggest that the latter position is overly pessimistic and that the former involves considerable overclassification. Basically, the great bulk of suicides all involve different manifestations of the vicissitudes of the sense of competence.

For example, Herbert Hendin's interesting little book, *Suicide and Scandinavia*, based mainly upon a small number of interviews carried out in Denmark, Norway, and Sweden, appears to accept as an initial postulate that there are different *kinds* of suicide in each of these countries. Implicitly rejecting the alternative hypothesis that the nature of suicide in the various countries is essentially similar, with the major differences being in the *extent* of the suicide-producing influences, he is impelled to seek and inflate marginal differences in the motives, mechanisms, and precipitating causes in the three countries. A number of his assertions, such as on the importance in Danish suicide of the need to rejoin in death a lost loved one, seem based upon scanty evidence and to miss their mark. A recent attempt by Block and Christiansen to test his hypotheses fails to offer support for a number of them. On a theoretical level, moreover, his contribution seems limited by the tenets of his particular school of psychiatry. Nonetheless, despite its overdifferentiation it contains a number of excellent psychiatric insights.

It will be noted that Freud, as well as a number of other theorists, makes rage the prime mover in suicide, whereas in the present theory it is a contributory force growing out of more basic processes. Freud maintained that the rage is turned inward in a kind of murder of the internalized parent figure, but the evidence for this is not convincing. Aggression adds energy to the impulse toward self-destruction; it is not its prime mover.

Clearly, the problem of suicide is not simply a matter of the management or the "direction" in which the aggression is turned. Individuals who have the kind of personality structure here described *generate more aggression* than healthy people and are then faced with the harrowing problem of handling it.

To recapitulate, it must be seen, then, that the administration of rage is no simple process. The rage becomes involved in a kind of special intensification: Lacking a basic sense of competence, the victim has a greater need than the healthy for supplies of nurturance. Consequently he hungers and clamors more furiously to elicit these supplies, antagonizes the potential grantor of supplies, and is thus the more deprived. But he does not dare express all his rage, so he is deprived of a chief weapon and feels the more incompetent. Moreover, he feels guilty at his rage and consequently the more worthless, incompetent, and self-punishing. In this emotional maelstrom unbearable pressures develop.

The evidence for the presence of aggression in suicide is overwhelming and widely documented. Frequently the suicidal act is carried out in a way that will inflict a maximum of pain upon the survivors, especially upon the one with whom the suicide is in symbiotic relationship. Suicide notes may express bitterness. In one suicide, for example, a man poisoned himself in a shallow closet so that when the door was opened his body fell forward upon the opener. In another, a man, pressed by his wife against his will to clean the attic, was discovered hanged in the cleaned attic. Ernest Hemingway blew off the top of his head while his wife was upstairs. Perhaps most revealing, my own research as well as that of others often found patients, just after regaining consciousness from a suicide attempt, expressing rage against someone close to them. Later, as controls strengthened, the rage disappeared.

Murder may be followed by suicide. Cases are constantly reported of one or more people being killed by a person who then turns the weapon on himself. In England, fully one-third of all murders are followed by suicide. Here the rage is fully expressed, with the consequent rush of guilt and the new untenability of the perpetrator's situation rendering the hopelessness and thus the pressure to commit suicide acutely greater.

My own studies in Norway and Denmark revealed a great variety of ways in which even normal Norwegians and Danes differ in their expression of aggression, thus providing further support for the hypothesis that personality factors are important in suicide and that these tend to permeate a whole culture. For example, in schoolyards during recess from classes Norwegian children were observed to engage in considerable horseplay, pushing, and physical contact. In Denmark this was much less common.

In general, indeed, Danes were observed to be more amiable and even-tempered, especially in public. One has the impression, too, of greater open aggression in the Norwegian culture in public controversy. The Norwegian press seems constantly to be reporting acrimonious disagreements and litigation, whereas this seems relatively rare in Denmark.

The Norwegian practice of *skippertak*, the procrastination of a task followed by an assault upon it, was discussed in connection with hope, which it certainly involves. At the same time, there is an element of aggression in *skippertak*, a kind of Viking storming of a position, a smashing of heads in the struggle with the task.

Norwegian literature, too, reflects the manner of handling aggression among these people. For example, in the novels of Knut Hamsun there are strong elements of expressed aggression in the backbreaking attack on a tough environment, in the boasting, in the open fighting, in the sharp practices.

A story by Hans Christian Andersen, "The Rags," is particularly interesting in that it is directly concerned with a comparison of the Norwegian and Danish characters. Speaking of the Danes, the Danish rag says "We are amiable and modest, we've too little faith in ourselves . . . I'm weak and yielding . . . I put up with everything." Here again, both the low feeling of competence and the long-suffering strangulation of resentment is observed.

Parties in Norway are more apt to involve people getting rapidly drunk and engaging, on occasion, in jousts of masculine physical strength, like high-kicking contests, in a kind of rough male struggle for mastery. Danish parties may be lively, but do not involve this kind of aggressive behavior.

There is, too, a greater tendency to boasting among the Norwegians, an aggressive assertion of superiority over others.

Thus, in many areas of life observed in Norway and Denmark these contrasts in aggressive expression emerge. Even the spoken languages seem to reflect this basic difference in personality style. The written languages of Norway and Denmark are almost identical, but they are spoken very differently. The "music" of Norwegian speech involves a sharp, assertive beat at the end of many words, whereas Danish is softer, more slurred, with, for example, the stop "d" softened to an "l."

The very methods of suicide themselves reflect the different characterological styles. Norwegians kill themselves most frequently by hanging, drowning, and firearms. The Danes much more frequently employ a less aggressive means—drugs.

A Gallup Poll finding is suggestive, although it involves a comparison of Denmark with England. Here it was found that, within the last twenty-four hours before the question was put, 26% of the

English had lost their tempers, while only 18% of the Danes had. When one considers that the English are themselves not particularly expressive of aggression, then this finding is eloquent.

Contemporary Danish painting, at least the samples I observed, can hardly be seen as aggressive. It is often soft and rather gentle, shrinking from bold and aggressive innovations, or is sometimes charmingly, childishly playful.

Yet the Danes do not totally succeed in suppressing their rage. While murders are indeed rare, when they do occur, they more often appear to be multiple or to involve a shocking bestiality. If the rage does fully break out, it reflects the pressure, as it were, of the severity with which it has been suppressed.

The quantitative questionnaire findings of my studies of Norwegians and Danes clearly confirm the basic observations on the greater expression of aggression among the Norwegians. For example:

Item: Some people, when injustice is done to them, tend to fight back very soon. Others suffer the injustices for quite some time and brood about them before perhaps finally exploding in anger.

As for myself:

	I react rather quickly	I react after a long time	I never really react
Norwegians:	78.7%	20.2%	1.1%
Danes:	61.3%	32.0%	4.4%

Item: I tend to become irritated quickly if things do not go well.

	Very true of me	Somewhat true of me
Norwegians:	26.4%	39.3%
Danes:	19.9%	29.8%

There are other less direct indications in the questionnaire data. If we make the plausible assumption that engaging in active sports represents something of a discharge of aggression, then the following is confirmatory:

Item: I engage frequently in active sports.

	Very true of me	Somewhat true of me
Norwegians:	28.7%	27.5%
Danes:	24.3%	14.9%

The following is congruent with the informal observations cited earlier:

Item: At parties I tend to become extremely gay and to forget myself completely.

	Very true of me	Somewhat true of me
Norwegians:	5.1%	31.5%
Danes:	3.9%	22.1%

Thus the empirical data, both quantitative and observational, support the hypothesis that national suicide rates reflect personality factors widespread in the cultures of these nations. Earlier, the empirical evidence was shown to support the hypothesis that the Danes are more vulnerable in their ability to sustain hope and weaker in their sense of competence. Here, such evidence reveals congruent differences in the management of aggression. Thus the findings tend also to undermine the position that suicide is due solely to external difficulties.

To recapitulate: Not everyone is an equal candidate for suicide. There are those who become the more readily hopeless in the face of the difficulties of life. These suffer basically from an impaired sense of competence, which has a chain of consequences that predispose, in an overdetermination of motives, to suicide.

4

The Blow and the Act

Suicide is usually precipitated by some event that constitutes a psychic blow. Earlier, we asserted that the blow is essentially a threat to acceptable life conditions and that it interacts with a low sense of competence to produce a low level of hope, in accordance with the formula:

$$S = f\left(\frac{T}{C}\right) = f\left(\frac{1}{H}\right)$$

in which S is the probability of Suicide, T is the Threat, C is the Sense of Competence, and H is Hope. It should now prove useful to examine more closely the nature and specific varieties of the blow.

We may note broadly at the outset that culture plays a role in determining what might constitute a blow. In Western Nigeria suicide may occur in the face of childlessness, sexual impotence, or weak libido. In some preliterate cultures an insult may precipitate suicide. Often, a taboo has been broken and when the transgressor is confronted and denounced he commits suicide. In Japan it still occurs that a person who has failed in his obligation to others may commit suicide, as in the recently reported case of a chief guard of a warehouse who felt he had not taken adequate emergency measures when a fire started in which nineteen firemen died. More typically in modern Japan, the precipitating cause may be failure on a crucial examination, refusal of the parents to approve a marriage, or desperate economic straits.

In our own culture, the findings in the following report on suicide causes for the city of San Francisco are fairly typical for the United States today. The list of precipitating causes in order of frequency is:

1. Poor health
2. Economic distress
3. Death of a loved one
4. Domestic difficulties

At first glance the broad array of precipitating causes in other cultures and in our own would seem to have little in common. What is asserted here is that basic to all these is the situation that *for a given low sense of competence the conditions of life have been rendered intolerable and unmanageable.*

In different cultures quite different values and failures of accomplishment may cause one to reach that point at which life seems unlivable, so that, as we have seen, the blows may differ. The value may be adequate sexual functioning and the production of offspring in some cultures, success in one's career in others. The content may differ; the essential assault does not. Thus, the breaking of a taboo in a primitive culture with subsequent denouement often involves tremendous withdrawal of social support and love, as well as a rush of shame, with the dual result of damaging the sense of competence and aggravating difficulties in the conditions of life.

Childlessness, where it is regarded as a sign of inadequacy, may clearly injure the sense of competence. Similarly, sexual impotence may be viewed as a lack of competence.

So, too, if we examine closely the major precipitating causes in our own culture. Poor health represents a rather pure case of a precipitating cause and a powerful one. Indeed it could be an effective cause in people whose vulnerability is not great. A continued painful illness, even partially disabling, when it becomes clear that it will probably never be cured, is virulently destructive of hope. The body image itself is diminished and impaired; the sense of competence is directly and intimately assaulted. Social difficulties may yet permit some avenues of hope—the loss of a loved one may possibly be remedied by finding a substitute—but the physically damaged or deteriorated organism patently will not improve. The extinction of hope is more overwhelming and that is why the suicidal act in such cases is apt to be more lethal. These people really wish to die and select a method than ensures it.

"Economic distress" is of course not a psychological term. Business reverses, prolonged unemployment, the loss of a job, failure to be promoted, all have powerful psychological consequences. The conditions of living have become difficult, but also the sense of competence is assaulted, again in people whose sense of competence, and consequently their ability to sustain hope, is fragile. This is supported by the fact that objectively it can often be shown that the suicide still had enough material resources to go on living at a reasonably comfortable economic level.

The loss of a loved one is felt as catastrophic by those vulnerable in their sense of competence. In the psychologically healthy there is, of course, grief and a period of mourning; but the grief heals. Life is still supportable. But in the vulnerable the response is that of the abandoned child. A symbiotic, dependent relation has existed with the loved one. Without him or her, one's own competence is felt to be insufficient to cope with life.

"Domestic difficulties" cover a variety of conflicts that constitute psychological blows to the sense of competence. Often they are conflicts between husbands and wives involving rage at the partner because of the frustration of dependent needs. Those damaged in their sense of competence usually enter marriage with unrealistic, insatiable expectations of succorance from their mates, which are of necessity disappointed. The vicious cycle of massive rage not fully expressed, of the threat of abandonment, of a constricted space of free movement—all further assaulting the sense of competence—is all too frequent. On occasion the relationship is between parents and grown children, with the psychodynamics not dissimilar.

Sometimes an apparently trivial event may appear to trigger a suicide. In one case I examined in Denmark, a daughter attempted suicide in a conflict with her mother over the use of a small piece of butter in the refrigerator. But this case and others with apparently trivial precipitating causes usually involve an event that is symbolic of some profound deprivation, or the event is perhaps just the last straw in destroying the sense of competence.

It should be clear of course that the final precipitating cause may well be a series of blows or a long ongoing one, like a chronic illness. There may also be a combination of blows, as when one is both ill and abandoned by a loved one, or when one fails in business and feels insufficiently supported by a wife.

To recapitulate, then, *it seems clear that in all these cases the precipitating cause is one that renders life more difficult to cope with and closes off any possibility of improvement in the situation, and that the difficulties are the kinds that strike most directly against the sense of competence.* They are difficulties with which the psychologically healthy might well cope; for those damaged in their sense of competence the interaction yields a desperately low level of hope.

If we return to the formula

$$S = f\left(\frac{T}{C}\right)$$

we observe that what occurs in suicide is that T, the Threat to acceptable life conditions, is high; C, the Sense of Competence, is low, resulting in a high value for S. In the psychologically healthy, for a given value of T, the value of C would be higher and the value of S, the probability of Suicide, therefore smaller.

As we have seen, if some present or anticipated state is perceived as destructive of acceptable life conditions, suicide may result. This state of affairs may be political, as in the case of the Buddhist monks in Viet Nam who set themselves afire in protest at the policies of the existing government. Here, to be sure, the aggressive component is strong, with the suicide intending his act to injure as much as possible the government he abominates.

So, too, the Japanese kamikaze pilots of World War II, who volunteered to ram their munitions-loaded planes into enemy battleships, must have perceived the loss of the war by Japan as insufferable. Again, there is an important aggressive component in the destruction of important enemy armaments and men.

In both types, the Buddhist monk and the kamikaze, the manipulative aspect is strong, for the act may help destroy or preclude the dreaded condition, though the suicide himself will not live to enjoy the results of his act. The beneficiary is some large group, such as the citizens of his country; and it is quite possible that this kind of suicide is more prevalent in cultures that have strong group ties and loyalties. These are not typical suicides; given the constellation of motives just described, such suicides may well take place in a mood of exaltation rather than in the more usual desperation and despair.

The Act

The final act of suicide is basically a resolution, a movement, perceived as the only possible one, out of a life situation felt to be unbearable by one of low sense of competence, with hope extinguished.

It is finally action, no longer just feeling. Often there seems to be an element of assertion here, an active rebellion against the passive acceptance of difficulties, a declaration of independence. It is as if the victim cries: "*At least I am competent to do this!*"

Human psychopathological acts are rarely based upon one pure unmixed motive and here, too, a number of motives that have emerged in the general analysis is evident. In some less serious attempts, with hope still flickering, the act is also a desperate "cry for help," as Shneidman and Farberow have called it, to those around. It may even be manipulatory and, as Stengel has pointed out, may succeed in getting from others what one wants. Serious suicidal acts also frequently contain a desire to manipulate the situation after death, as evidenced by the fairly frequent detailed instructions to survivors in suicide notes.

There may also be involved the "gamble with death," the testing of the environment, in which the victim may or may not be saved, depending upon the concern of those around. The neglected wife may take an overdose of sleeping pills which will kill her if she is left undisturbed, but from which she could be saved if her husband should come home rather than spend the evening with his mistress.

Frequently, as we have seen, aggression is strikingly evident in the mélange of motives. Some of the rage against those who are seen as not helping sufficiently, usually among those emotionally close to the subject, breaks through in the manner or conditions of the act.

Finally, in those cases in which the rage has produced massive guilt, there may be elements of expiation in the suicidal act. The act partakes of self-punishment. Under these circumstances, if the attempt does not result in death, the subject may be drained of guilt by the self-punishment of the act, and the pressure toward suicide relieved. For some, this process has something of the character of a rebirth, as one faces life anew, freed of punishing guilt.

At the time of the act, alcohol may play a part. In the drunken state normal inhibitions are weakened and those disposed toward suicide may more easily act upon their suicidal impulses. In some cultures alcohol may play a relatively important role: The Finnish investigator Verkho believes that the extremely high Finnish suicide rates are traceable to the particularly disastrous consequences of mixing the Finnish character with alcohol. In any case, alcohol cannot be seen as a primary precipitating cause; it lubricates the path of suicidal impulses already present.

The Techniques of Suicide

What of the actual method used by the victim to end his life? Does it have any systematic or theoretical interest? We may note, first of all, that there may be a cultural tradition with regard to it, a "standard" method in a particular culture. In one South Pacific culture almost all the suicides climb a high palm and leap off.

In Tikopia the suicide paddles or swims into the great reaches of the Pacific. There may be subcultural traditions, like leaping off the Golden Gate Bridge in San Francisco, or off a Lover's Leap cliff in some communities. Where a cultural tradition is strong, a particular method may be identified with the very thought of committing suicide.

Somewhat related to tradition, but to a considerable degree independent of it, is the factor of sheer ready availability of a particular means. Jumping off a tall palm may also be the most available method in a tropical country. A firearm constantly close at hand is apt to be used by someone when he decides upon suicide. Policemen, for example, tend to use their pistols to commit suicide. Household knives and poisons may be used by housewives.

Availability may be just about the sole determinant of the choice of method in situations in which the victim is at a particular time overwhelmingly bent upon suicide under sharply restricted conditions. In a prison cell or in a mental hospital enormous ingenuity is often shown in finding or adapting something to suicidal purposes, such as breaking one's eyeglasses and using the broken glass to cut the wrists, and other more bizarre adaptations.

There are historical changes in methods. Some methods highly frequent not long ago have declined; new ones have appeared. Earlier in this century, for example, ordinary illuminating gas was frequently used, often by putting one's head in the oven and turning on the gas. Recently there has been a sharp increase in the use of various pills, such as barbiturates and tranquilizers. Changing availability is, of course, an important factor in historical changes in methods.

To some slight degree there are even fads in suicidal methods. Several years ago it was discovered that suffocation could rapidly be induced by putting a transparent plastic bag over one's head. This was followed by a small wave of suicides using this method.

Most interesting and revealing psychologically is the fact that the choice of method may be determined by, and therefore reveal something of, the motives and personality of the suicide. It is perhaps too much to say that this is *always* so, as did Wilhelm Stekel, but some acts seem clearly revealing. A suicide may be arranged, as we have seen, so that it inflicts in its rage a maximum of distress upon the survivors. Or, on the other hand, where rage is strongly repressed, the suicide may be arranged to look like an accidental death, thereby sparing the survivors to a considerable degree.

Methods motivated by strong self-hatred may involve violent mutilations of the victim. In physical illness, sometimes the suicidal attack seems to be directly upon the part of the body where unbearable pain exists, a direct assault against the pain, as in stabbing the abdomen in the hurting area.

It is congruent with our general analysis that the most frequent Norwegian suicide method is hanging, a rather aggressive and violent method, whereas the most frequent Danish method is taking pills, the less aggressive and more passive method. To some degree, at least, cultures tend to employ methods of suicide that reflect the nature of their vulnerability.

5

The First Wounds

The evidence is by now strong that the damage in the adult personality that renders it susceptible to suicide has its origins early in life. Freud, of course, was the first to develop systematically the idea of infantile and childhood origins of mental disturbance. His evidence, however, was largely retrospective and reconstructive rather than based upon direct studies of the young. More recently, however, investigations of infants and young children by such researchers as Spitz, Bowlby, and others, have provided more direct evidence for such early damage. That some of these studies may have methodological imperfections does not detract significantly from the heavy weight of evidence they cumulatively provide.

Several recent studies are directly relevant to the problem of suicide. An investigation by Greer, Gunn, and Koller showed that a group of adults who had attempted suicide had a more frequent history of childhood parental loss, which occurred at an earlier age, and which was less often replaced by substitutes, than did nonsuicidal control groups.

A study by Assael of a group of women who showed a preoccupation with death and suicide all their lives and who, in the main, actually committed suicide in early adulthood, showed that they tended to have rejecting mothers and that they had early severe feeding problems, often with tendencies toward marasmus, that curious wasting-away disease of infants.

A study by Schrut of suicides among children and adolescents reveals a high frequency of rejecting mothers. Often, Schrut found, the rejection is not total, but torn by ambivalence.

It must be stated at the outset that there is no unanimous agreement as to precisely how and through what psychodynamics these injuries take place. There are theoretical differences among the Freudians, the Melanie Klein group, various neo-Freudian groups, and the academic American empiricists. We clearly do not as yet fully understand all the complex influences in early life that go to make up what we call the personality. It does seem possible, nevertheless, from a closer examination of the evidence, to construct a viable general formulation of the nature of the injury.

The process of wounding is an intricate one. The earliest wounds create distorted perceptions and defenses that render the child more vulnerable to later stress and therefore to later wounding. Moreover, the behavior of the wounded child may elicit irritation and rejection in the parent, leading into a vicious cycle of "bad" behavior, to rejection, to worse behavior and so, deplorably, on. Here I shall concentrate upon those influences that seem most closely related to the sense of competence and to suicide.

The first basic generalization concerning the injury that can be made is that *there is a disruption in the symbiotic relationship between mother and infant*. It becomes increasingly clear that the natural and necessary environment of the infant is characterized by a nurturant mother. Complex sets of mutual expectations and signals develop between infant and mother that must become harmoniously orchestrated if the infant is to develop normally. There are doubtless developmental phases during which the interrelations and vulnerabilities change. There is some evidence that disruptions in the first six months are of a different nature and have different consequences than those in the second six months, when there is more identification of the mother and social interplay. Erik Erikson has well described the basic trust that develops in the infant in the first year if the relationship is harmonious and the basic mistrust if disruption takes place.

The major cause of symbiotic disruption is in all probability prolonged abandonment of the infant by the mother. Infants respond initially to the absence of a mother figure with crying and rage, but after prolonged abandonment the desperate efforts to re-establish the relationship are given up in a kind of despair.

The abandonment may not always be obvious. Institutionalized infants may be receiving adequate physical care, but the shifting pattern of caretakers, their meager contact with the infant, and the routinization of feeding leaves the infant with no particular mother figure to whom it can signal its needs and with whom it can establish a healthy symbiotic relationship. Spitz speaks of the development of an "anaclitic depression" in institutionalized children, which may be the primitive prototype of depression in adults. Such cases of disruption may also result in marasmus, the physical wasting-away of the infant, marked by refusal to eat and almost always subsequent death.

A hypothesis suggests itself here that may be presented only with great tentativeness. It is that *even in the infant, when the conditions for coping successfully with life appear hopeless, there is an accelerated turning toward death.* In the infant it cannot be said to be a deliberately chosen act but rather that it happens in a primitive, almost automatic way. The struggle to live is given up, there is a kind of depression with attendant antivital biochemical processes, there may be refusal to eat, and holding of the breath.

Interestingly, Harlow and his associates have observed self-destructive behavior, such as self-biting, in young monkeys raised without mothers. The suggestion made here is that deep-seated in the species, when conditions for living become hopeless, there is a tendency to bring on death more rapidly than might occur if the struggle continued until the very end. Perhaps here lie the ultimate biosocial foundations, the primitive prototypes of depression and suicide.

Weaning in itself is probably not as important as the early psychoanalysts believed. It may be part of a larger process, however, which could be crucial. For example, if early and sudden weaning takes place as part of a more general abandonment by the mother, the effects may be disastrous. But a gentle shift from breast to bottle within a protective context need not be. Devereux reports that among the Mohave Indians an infant may die following its forced sudden weaning, which apparently involves considerable rejection, following a new pregnancy by the mother. Curiously, the Mohave believe that the infant knows that the mother is pregnant and commits suicide through becoming ill. This belief, far from being merely an ignorant misinterpretation, could contain an acute insight.

What is involved is the variable hope, in its most basic sense of referring to the outlook for one's very life. It is at these early levels that a certain fragility of hope may be established, a mistrust of the environment, a disbelief that it will behave in a salutory way, a tendency to become more easily hopeless in the face of threats.

But hope itself is based upon something even more fundamental, the basic sense of competence. It will be recalled that:

$$\text{Hope} = f\left(\frac{\text{Sense of Competence}}{\text{Threat}}\right)$$

Under a given Threat, then, the level of Hope will be low if the Sense of Competence is low. And indeed, it is this sense of competence that is the fundamental human quality that is injured by symbiotic disruption.

In the childhood years beyond infancy, one of the most direct and virulent destroyers of the sense of competence is *disparagement* by parents. If a child is defined as helpless and incompetent by his apparently omniscient parents, he can hardly help but internalize their definition.

A second destructive influence is the induction of *guilt* in the child. The aggression expressed by children when their dependent demands are not met can be highly disturbing to mothers; and it is not surprising that many mothers attempt to control the child's aggression by making him feel that he has committed some unforgivable act which now renders him basically bad and worthless, a state that might be alleviated only by extensive expiation. As with disparagement, the definition becomes internalized. The feeling that now one does not *deserve* the good things of the world adds to the sense of deprivation, weakness, and incompetence.

Mothers often emit contradictory signals and expectations that can be acutely disturbing to children. A mother whose expression and posture reveal that she is really furious with her child may nonetheless speak simultaneously in loving tones and words, to the child's profound confusion. She may punish a child for a given act in private but, for appearances' sake, tolerate it in public. One effect can be the child's decision that he is incapable of interpreting signals from other humans, with an enormously destructive effect upon his sense of competence.

A central problem in the development of children is that of identification with a parent figure. In the healthy situation the child eventually identifies with the parent of the same sex. Moreover, this parent constitutes a model of competent functioning in the family and in the culture. The strong arousal of guilt in a little boy by his mother may force him into a compulsive identification with her. The presence in the home of a weak and ineffectual father provides no role model for competence in a boy. Thus the problem of successful identity definition is closely linked with the sense of competence.

In this connection, a study by Heinicke reveals that for boys whose level of guilt is high the mothers are central, whereas for boys with a low level of guilt the fathers are central; this tends to confirm the relationship between unsuccessful identification and guilt.

Finally, it should be clear that maternal deprivation, the "abandonment" of children by mothers, continues to have powerful effects beyond infancy and through the period of childhood, arousing feelings of helplessness and despair.

These, then, constitute some of the major influences in childhood that appear to produce personalities wounded in their sense of competence, who might later, under certain trying circumstances, be victims of suicide.

My investigations in high-suicide Denmark and low-suicide Norway support the hypothesis that Danish infant-care practices are more conducive to disruption of the mother-infant relationship than are Norwegian.

I was struck by a fundamental difference in the two countries. The Norwegians bend all efforts to keep mother and child together. The Danes, in contrast, tend to view motherhood as a burden on the mother from which all efforts should be made to relieve her.

There is a strong feminist segment of Danish culture which tends to minimize sex differences and to feel that women have been exploited. A Danish friend, a feminist of formidable charm and energy, informed me that she was able, for a while, to persuade a group of men (ah, Vikings!) to sit around darning socks in a kind of equalization of tasks between the sexes. Norwegian feminism has not taken quite this form.

The basic contrast in child-rearing practices between Denmark and Norway is manifested in many ways. The following are notable:

1. Weaning of infants takes place considerably earlier in Denmark than in Norway. Toilet training is also reported to be earlier. These practices reflect broader differences in values and practices.

2. The proportion of working mothers is many times higher in Denmark than in Norway. Moreover, Danish mothers have their highest rate of employment during their childbearing years. Many Danish mothers of infants are working. (The United States also has a high proportion of working women, but these tend to consist mainly of the pre- and post-childbearing age groups, with the childbearing age groups tending not to work.)

3. There are a great many infant day nurseries in Denmark; there are very few in Norway. The main function of the Danish nursery is to leave the mothers free to work during the day. The baby is deposited in the morning and picked up late in the afternoon. (Sometimes the crying baby is left on the nursery steps before it opens in the morning because the mother must begin work early.)

4. Institutions for the *full-time* care of infants are far more frequent in Denmark than in Norway.

These Danish institutions differ among themselves in their practices, but at least some carry on procedures which have been demonstrated to have disruptive effects upon infants. Some are extremely strict, believing in principle that babies should be allowed to cry themselves blue in the face rather than be picked up and comforted.

In one institution that I investigated, which received babies at birth, the superintendent informed me proudly that it was their policy never to release a baby for adoption before the age of two and one-half years, "to be sure that they are healthy." She had no inkling that the sickness of some of her babies may have resulted, ironically, from her own benevolent treatment. There were thirty babies in this small institution at the time of my visit, of which five were mentally defective, an extraordinarily high percentage. One wonders if any of these might not have been cases of infantile depression brought on by the institutional regimen.

A study by Simonsen in Denmark suggests that children's homes are more destructive than day nurseries, where the children spend only part of their time. Children in the children's homes were found to be less spontaneously creative, poorer in language development, and to have a lower general Developmental Quotient of maturity of behavior.

A Danish psychiatrist, Dr. Hedwig Jacoby, who has been studying the effects of early institutionalization, reports that the effects of such treatment before the age of three months results in children who are excessively dependent, who cling undiscriminatingly to adults, and who cannot adjust later to adoption. These may or may not grow up to be potential suicides, but they do illustrate the destructive effects of maternal deprivation. Later deprivations are in all probability also involved in the production of the potentially suicidal.

There are other possible indicators that suggest a certain deficiency in succorance of babies in Denmark. An observer of the Danish scene reports frequently seeing crying babies left unattended in their carriages, with passersby showing no concern. One is struck, too, by the rather frequent Danish practice of carting babies about a traffic-filled city in baskets at the back of bicycles, which may reveal a certain cavalier attitude toward the baby's safety.

5. When we examine the situation of young children beyond infancy, we note, first, that schools for preschool children are far more numerous in Denmark than in Norway, again indicating greater separation of mother and child in Denmark.

Further, observers acquainted with such schools report that the basic function of the schools is rather different in the two countries. The Norwegian schools are mainly educational; the children spend perhaps four hours per day there. The Danish schools are, like the baby nurseries, mainly designed to relieve working mothers. The children are left early and stay late, to be picked up after work. In general, the Danish schools are stricter, with fewer self-demand tasks. Again we see the greater separation of mother and child and, moreover, a suppression of spontaneity that cannot but have an injurious effect upon the sense of competence.

Danish child rearing is perhaps more authoritarian than it wishes to be. Mothers disapprove of being authoritarian, but they slip into it in exasperation. So, too, they may strike their children, but almost never in public. Appearances must be kept up. Significantly, devaluation, Danish child psychologists report, is much used to control children.

Danish mothers are reported to attempt to hide their anger while talking nicely to a misbehaving child, thus emitting conflicting and confusing signals as well as providing a model for the suppression of rage. Aggression in the child is often treated by making it feel guilty. Expression of aggression is in general frowned upon.

I would maintain that all these—the authoritarian attack upon self-reliance, the inconsistency in signals and expectations, the use of devaluation, the fostering of guilt, the suppression of aggression—all these constitute *attacks upon the sense of competence.* (It is significant that school phobia is a common difficulty among Danish children, representing their helpless clinging to the mother because of a low sense of competence.)

These influences seem to be lacking, or at least are only mildly present, in Norwegian child rearing. Norwegian mothers tend to concentrate heavily on the care of their babies to an extent that appears to arouse resentment in many Norwegian husbands. Indeed, some descriptions of Norwegian child rearing are so idyllic that they are somewhat suspect. In one study of a central mountain community, it is reported that children are much loved, rarely disciplined, highly indulged, and that the mother is always present. The parental models openly express aggression, at least verbally, in their hostile talk about some commonly disliked person. Another study speaks of the "notable ease, freedom, and relaxed independence of Norwegian youngsters as they grow up, despite school discipline."

One striking feature that emerged from my own data concerns the role of the father. The Norwegian father looms large in the family. He is seen as a figure of strength. He may well spend time training and encouraging his little sons. The Danish father does not play so strong a role; the mothers appear to be more central. For example, our data show:

Item: When I was a small child, my father was very strict with me.

Percentage Agreeing:

Norwegians:	27.0
Danes:	12.2

The Danish father does not present a strong figure with whom a son can identify. Himself apt to be injured in his sense of competence and therefore basically rather dependent, not expected by his culture to manifest more than pleasant affability, he is not likely to provide a model of strength. The Norwegian father, in contrast, both in his psychodynamics and in the expectations for his role in the culture, more frequently presents a figure of some strength and independence.

Moreover, these Danish fathers, themselves somewhat dependent, often fail to satisfy the dependency needs of their wives. These wives, as mothers, may then in their frustration express their aggression in rejection of their children. As wives, they may express their dissatisfaction in disparagement of the husband, rendering him less acceptable as a model.

The description of child-rearing practices in a culture must almost invariably involve oversimplification and overgeneralization. My studies of child rearing, based upon direct observation, the questionnaire findings, interviews with Danish and Norwegian experts, and a survey of the research literature, doubtless suffer from these strictures. Moreover, some of the healthier features of Danish child rearing are not discussed here, given our special interest in suicide, but rather some of the more pathological manipulations. These are doubtless found in other cultures as well, but it is a matter of degree and of the particular constellation.

Suicidal people, it has been asserted here, are in the main people who have been psychologically wounded. We are able to say something of the processes of wounding, even if not able to describe them with precision. In support of this analysis, it is possible to demonstrate that a high-suicide country engages in far more of these wound-producing practices than does a low-suicide country, and that the nature of the wounds is precisely that which the theory maintains is productive of later suicide.

6

The Social Surround

In the complex welter of activities, relationships, and institutions that constitutes the social life of man, suicide rates have been shown to be associated with a large number of variables. Relatively high suicide rates have been reported to be associated with, for example:

Male sex
Older age
White race membership (vs. Negro) in the U.S.
Urbanization
High population density
Protestantism
Peacetime (versus wartime)
Economic depression
Socially disorganized areas of cities
Upper social classes
Certain occupations
Countries with low homicide rates

The list could be prolonged, but it is sufficiently illustrative. Several things must be noted about these variables and the nature of their relation to suicide. Clearly, a number of them overlap; for example, race with social class, urbanization with socially disorganized areas of cities. As concepts they derive from various disciplines based upon different classificatory principles, some economic, some broadly demographic, some more narrowly analytic. Moreover, the relationships are of a low order. The rates are noteworthy in contrast to those of other groups of even lower rates, but the absolute magnitudes of the rates are low. As a proportion of the respective category, very few Protestants kill themselves, or males, or members of the white race.

Consequently, the rubric of "exceptions" to these relationships contains the great bulk of cases. And we are left with the awkward task of explaining why, overwhelmingly, Protestants, and males, and members of the white race do *not* commit suicide.

Even at a level at which the relationship is fairly high, such as that Catholic countries tend to have lower rates than Protestant countries, startling exceptions disrupt any easy social-theory-building: Catholic France has a relatively high rate, Protestant Norway and the Netherlands have low rates.

Finally, we must note that the relationships are historically unstable. The contrast between urban and rural suicide rates seems to be disappearing: In the United States it is no longer striking, and in Denmark some rural areas actually have higher rates than the adjoining towns.

The crucial point about all these relationships is that they are *distal* ones. Their relation to the act of suicide is often obscure, usually passing through a number of intermediary causal links about which we can only make educated guesses. "Negroness" has no direct relation to suicide; rather there are complex social and psychological linkages not entirely dissected out. The uncovering of such distal relationships is the beginning of social science. They stimulate the generation of hypotheses (in itself valuable) and may even have some actuarial predictive power; but the difficult and necessary job is the uncovering of the intermediate linkages and the discovery of the ultimate proximal ones.

For the heart of the social science enterprise and probably of the whole scientific enterprise is the uncovering of the best-fitting *proximal* variables influencing the events one is studying. If scientific laws can be extracted concerning the social universe, they will, I believe, have to consist of such proximal variables. That has been the effort of this book.

More than any other group, it is the sociologists who have been concerned with the development of a theory of suicide. More than a half-century ago, Emile Durkheim, a pioneer of sociology, presented his influential theory of suicide. Daringly, Durkheim attempted to remain on the level of collectivities, to view suicide as a product of certain kinds of societies, without reference to the individuals constituting them. "Social integration" was his central concept, which he maintained to be inversely related to suicide rates, with the various types of suicide being associated with variations in social integration.

One major difficulty with the theory is in determining some measure of social integration. For "integration" is a general term, and human interrelationships are too varied and complex to be so easily categorized. Could one assign unequivocal social integration ratings to the world's societies?

Another serious difficulty was introduced by Durkheim's principled attempt to remain in the level of collectivities, a distal level indeed. By precluding the individual *a priori*, he blinded himself to individual determinants, leaving himself with a theory that had little power to explain suicide. His explanation for the relatively high suicide rate of the divorced, for example, could be only that after the divorce they were no longer members of an integrated group, notably the family. He did not see that the divorced were also apt to be psychologically different from the married, that they were a different population more apt to have been psychologically disturbed people to begin with. The sociologist Alex Inkeles has also noted this fallacy.

Sociological theories of suicide, in the main, fail to perceive that their categories may contain high concentrations of certain personality types. They ascribe causality exclusively to factors usually quite distal in the social surround, which have in fact but feeble explanatory power.

Since Durkheim, a number of sociological theories of suicide have been produced, all primarily concerned with distal relationships. Cavan, for example, in 1928, reflecting the orientation of the Chicago school of her time, found disorganized areas of the city to be the major determinant of suicide.

More recently, Peter Sainsbury, basing his conclusions upon a careful ecological study of the distribution of suicide in London, observed—not surprisingly, by 1955—that the major factors were social isolation, social mobility, and social disorganization. Unlike Durkheim, however, who maintained a gallant purity in remaining on the level of collectivities, Sainsbury attempts a direct leap to a proximal level by suggesting that the loneliness of life in the boroughs of boarding houses and high social mobility is the more direct cause. To be sure, loneliness is a factor in some suicides, but a close examination of the life history of the lonely often reveals that it is the end product of a long chain of inability to relate satisfactorily to others. Despite his own evidence that the high-suicide boroughs are characterized by a tremendous rate of daily turnover in residence, he rejects the notion that the psychologically disturbed might be heavily represented among these mobile persons. How did it come about that a man is living alone and temporarily in a bed-sitter in Holborn rather than with a wife and children in a small house in Deptford?

It is cruelly ironic, too, that social isolates are often the very kind of personalities who can least tolerate social isolation. They have an insatiable hunger for receiving love from others but have antagonized them by the extravagance of their demands and by their rage, directly and indirectly expressed, all of which has contributed to their social isolation.

The Danish investigator Kirsten Rudfeld has suggested, as a result of her studies in Denmark, that the infrequency of secondary social contacts is the major factor in suicide. Again we have a distal variable, many obscure links from the act of suicide. Indeed, it is a feeble variable, for the Danish suicide rate has been high for the last hundred years despite the great shift in frequency from primary to secondary contacts as industrialization and urbanization developed. If Rudfeld's theory had any significant power, the Danish suicide rate would have risen sharply over the last century.

There are also several sociological theories based upon social status as the major determinant. This, too, is in itself a variable of no great power, for the relation between social class and suicide is slight, with somewhat higher rates sometimes reported in the upper classes. A downward change in social status might be a more powerful variable since it impinges on the sense of competence; but without a distorted generalization of the concept of social status beyond its valid meaning, it can account for little in the variance of suicide rates. Theories that attempt to employ certain properties of social status, such as the status integration theory of Gibbs, are equally feeble in explanatory power.

Doubtless the most elaborate and ambitious attempt to develop a theory of suicide has been made by Henry and Short. They counterpose suicide and homicide and postulate what they consider to be the major variables determining each. Basic for them are the concepts of external and internal restraints, these being related to position in the status hierarchy and the degree of relational environment. It is asserted that high external restraints, which are associated with intense involvement in social relations with others, lead to blaming others for difficulties, to turning aggression outward, and thus to high homicide rates and low suicide rates, with the opposites of these conditions leading to the reverse.

There are, I would suggest, grave failures in this theory. The concepts of external and internal restraints are so broad and vague that they are difficult to apply to the complex realities of human societies. Social restraints are subtle, varied, and not easily describable. Moreover, if one looks at actual societies, the postulated relationships turn out to be false. For example, Japan, where disapproval of others plays a powerful role and shaming may be considered one of the predominent means of social control, would appear to be a country of high external restraints, yet it has a high suicide rate, contrary to the theory.

The application of the theory to reality seems frequently faulty. It asserts that the lower classes are more strongly subjected to external restraints, but this is arguable. In fact, much behavior, both sexual and aggressive, is tolerated in the lower classes that is not tolerated in higher classes.

The linkage of "intense involvement in social relations with others" with low suicide rates seems also to fly in the face of reality. Indeed, suicides are often among the most intensely involved in social relations with others. Since many are highly dependent people they are often involved with great intensity and, as in domestic quarrels and love affairs leading to suicide, the involvement is at the heart of their problems. Even the lonely and isolated have intense involvements from which they have become physically separated.

Curiously, the theory makes use of the proximal, psychoanalytic notions of the turning inward or outward of aggression; but it links them, rather inelegantly, not with other proximal variables to which they properly adhere but to the distal ones of the theory.

Another psychological variable used by Henry and Short is the "flow of love" in a society or groups, which they assert is productive of suicide. In this form the concept is so vague and unspecified as to be difficult to interpret. Actually, in the main, quite the opposite seems to be true. If the flow of love is a nurturant support by those around one, then it is antisuicidal. If the flow of love is the loving care of a mother for her child so that it grows into a psychologically healthy adult, then it too is antisuicidal. Certain special circumstances, in which the flow of love to a child is interrupted and its permanent loss threatened in its training and discipline, can be seen as productive of suicide-prone adults. This can hardly be categorized as the flow of love, but rather is something closer to its opposite.

In summing up, then, it would seem that a close examination of the theory or any attempt to apply it leads to an intellectual morass. Distal theories, of which this is the most elaborate, are either flatly wrong, feeble, or both. They may be of use, but they are not at the heart of the matter.

A promising strategy of theory construction would appear to be to work back from, but close to, the proximal variables in the direction of distal social ones, rather than producing the intellectual chasms of distal relationships. Using such an approach, what social variables lie close to the proximal ones determining the act of suicide? Referring only to the social surround and thus excluding the personality structure that is susceptible to suicide, what variables have high, proximal relations to suicide?

One such variable is the *lack of succorant persons and institutions.* A "cold" society, which shows little concern for people in trouble, either from primary or secondary groups, will, other things being equal, have a high suicide rate. I would suggest as a hypothesis that the warmth of primary group succorance is a contributing factor to the low suicide rate of the Irish, the Italians, and, perhaps, the Norwegians.

There is some quantitative support for this hypothesis in our questionnaire findings in Norway and Denmark.

Item: In some countries it is customary for neighbors to help each other. In other countries neighbors keep more to themselves. In the case of my family I would say they:

	Are fairly helpful to neighbors	Keep to themselves
Norwegians:	41.6%	21.9%
Danes:	27.6%	37.6%

On the other hand, a contributing factor to the high rates in Skid Rows and disorganized areas of cities could well be the "coldness" of the social surround. We have seen, however, that here personality predispositions in all probability play an important interactive role.

A lack of succorance is doubtless one component of loneliness, which is often cited as a cause of suicide. The social isolate is not apt to be the object of much warm human giving. The feeling of loneliness, however, does not correlate perfectly with the degree of social isolation; the possessor of friends and acquaintances can also feel lonely. It is the person damaged in his sense of competence, the dependent personality, who is apt to crave human contact most acutely and who experiences loneliness most poignantly. The lack of succorance, therefore, must be conceptualized as interacting with the personality variable in our theoretical formulations.

A second proximal social variable, related to the lack of succorance but separable from it, is that of the existence in the society of *strong demands for the exercising of competence.* This covers a wide range of behavior; for example, it includes demands that people behave in "strong" nondependent fashion. The many who cannot are thus seen as, and see themselves as, failures and incompetent. I would suspect this to be a factor in the high Swedish, German, and Japanese suicide rates as well as an important factor in the United States.

A third proximal social variable, related to but separable from the others, is that of *demands for interpersonal giving.* It will be recalled that those injured in their sense of competence are apt to be psychologically dependent and unable easily to give succorance to others. Yet there are social roles and occupations which, at least in certain societies and at certain periods in history, by their very nature demand enormous outlays of concern and nurturance to others. The practice of medicine in the United States at this time is one such occupation. So, too, is nursing. And so, too, is that of the self-employed proprietor, pushed beyond his ability in catering to customers. *All these occupations have high suicide rates.*

That these high rates do not result from working hard or exerting oneself can be seen from the fact that in high-suicide Denmark the rate for fishermen is low, and in the United States it is low for such occupations as truck driver, carpenter, and mechanic.

This concept of interpersonal giving appears to have considerable explanatory power. Sociologists have noted occupational relations to suicide rates but have not been able satisfactorily to explain them. Social-status theories, for example, are totally unsuccessful. It is to the demands for interpersonal giving in an occupation that we must look.

Another characteristic of the social surround that predisposes to suicide might be called *the lack of a hopeful future time perspective,* or, closely related, a constricted psychological space of free movement. The contrast here is between societies in which few hopeful avenues are open and those in which hopes can be powerfully engaged. Vienna, particularly between the two world wars, seems to have been a society that offered few avenues for those grasping at hope, and it had a high suicide rate. East Berlin, too, in recent years and for somewhat other reasons has supplied few hopes and it, too, has a high rate. We have noted that underdeveloped countries that are developing rapidly might be expected to have low rates.

There is one social variable that is almost self-evident, yet it is one that cannot be excluded. That is, *the degree of toleration of suicide in the society*, or, put the other way, the degree of its prohibition. The strong disapproval of suicide by the Catholic Church in countries like Italy, Spain, and Ireland in all probability contributes to the low suicide rates in these countries, although the reported statistics must be viewed with considerable caution. My own statistics suggest that the variable may play a role in the Norwegian-Danish differences in suicide rates, revealing that Danes are more tolerant of suicide than are Norwegians:

Item: People have different opinions about the morality of suicide. Please check the one that comes closest to your own.

	Norwegians:	Danes:
One has a perfect right to commit suicide if one wishes to, regardless of circumstances.	10.2%	14.9%
While I tend to deplore suicide, I am tolerant of people's right to commit it if they feel they must.	24.7%	40.3%
Only under rare and very extreme circumstances might there be any justification for committing suicide.	41.6%	28.2%
Suicide is morally wrong, and no one has a right to commit suicide under any circumstances.	22.5%	12.7%

These appear to me to be some of the major variables of the social surround that are fairly proximal to the act of suicide. Moving cautiously out from them, one might establish via several links the chains leading to the kind of distal variables listed at the beginning of this chapter.

Stated more formally, on the level of analysis of the relatively proximal social surround:

$$S = f\left(\frac{DEC, DIG, TS}{Su, HFT}\right)$$

In which S is the probability of Suicide, DEC the Demands for the Exercising of Competence, DIG the Demand for Interpersonal Giving, TS the Tolerance of Suicide, Su the availability of Succorance, and HFT the degree of Hope in the Future Time Perspective.

We must not forget, of course, that the direction of the flow of influence is not only from the social surround to the individual. In one sense individuals inherit their society, but they also create and modify it. Danish society, for example, may be seen not only as constituting a social surround but also as being a creation expressive of Danish personality and its needs. As if to compensate and provide for the gnawing emotional hunger deep in many Danes, Danish society is externally indulgent. There is the highly developed benign welfare state providing its nurturance. There are abundant supplies of good food and drink and the indulgence in them. There is considerable sexual indulgence. An affable, cozy, indulgent society would seem to have been created, bountiful to its ever-hungry children.

A number of developments in the history of Denmark could have been forerunners of those conditions in contemporary Denmark that are particularly relevant to suicide. One of these is the decline of Denmark as a formidable European power, culminating in her defeat by Prussia in 1864. The spiritual rehabilitation of Denmark under the influence of Bishop Grundtvig involved a turning inward of energies formerly involved in wars and the expression of aggression. This could well have involved a greater restrictiveness in child rearing aimed at self-control, particularly of aggression, with resultant damage to the sense of competence.

An earlier possible influence, suggested to me by the Norwegian writer Finn Carling, was the Danish institution of *stavnsbånd*, which prevented by law the leaving of farms by the farmer's children. One might speculate that this necessitated repressive child rearing to minimize friction in the closely knit group. Norway did not have this institution.

It might be noted, too, that although contemporary Denmark is on the whole less religious than contemporary Norway, somewhat earlier, in the eighteenth century, Danish religion was considerably more strict and guilt-ridden than Norwegian. Possibly, submerged elements of this guilt continue to play some role in Danish culture.

One might note, too, that life in Denmark did not involve as harsh a struggle with nature as in Norway and that possibly the Danish culture therefore did not require the production of personalities capable of outward aggression for this struggle.

Then there is the Danish tradition of civic "goodness." That is, Danes are excellent citizens, concerned that the state and its institutions work well. They obey regulations; they do not cross streets against the traffic lights. The price paid for this may again be a restriction in child rearing, greater need for self-control, and stronger social pressures.

The Danish student of suicide Schiødt, who has investigated suicide rates in the various regions of Denmark, has suggested that the presence of foreign troops has played an important role, but it appears rather difficult to draw plausible connections here.

It must be stressed again that these are not presented as causes of suicide, but only as speculations about possible historical developments that may have been of some influence in laying down conditions that were the forerunners of the present state of affairs.

The Welfare State

The assertion has frequently been made that the welfare state, characterized by the provision of various social security services for its citizens, results in increased suicide rates. The issue produced something of a minor international scandal when, some years ago, former President Eisenhower referred in a speech to a "friendly European nation," which, as a consequence of "almost complete paternalism," had experienced a sharp rise in suicides, "more than twice our drunkenness," and "a lack of moderation discernable on all sides."

Since there are massive trends throughout the world, in countries with a wide range of political ideologies, toward the welfare state, it is important to seek a definitive answer to this question.

Those who assert this relationship usually present one or more of the following explanations: The welfare state destroys individual incentive, fosters boredom, and thus destroys the zest for living. The soft life encouraged by the welfare state fails to develop in people the toughness necessary to withstand life's difficulties, so that even minor troubles may lead to suicide. The arguments are not usually couched in psychologically sophisticated terms. In the language of relatively established concepts of psychology, the hypothesis would appear to entail the notions that, first, major motives toward continuing one's life are diminished in intensity through diminution in the attractiveness of the future time-perspective, and, second, that the adaptation level for frustration is lowered.

The problem was investigated as part of the larger study. The major relevant findings are as follows:

1. Norway is a welfare state, yet it has a low suicide rate (roughly, 7 per 100,000).
2. Denmark has had a high suicide rate for over one hundred years (roughly 20–30 per 100,000), long before it became a welfare state. The Danish rate did not rise with the advent of the welfare state. If anything, it showed a moderate decline.
3. In Denmark, there was a drop in the suicide rate for old people following the establishment of these extensive social security practices. For males age sixty-five and over, the rate dropped from 150 per 100,000 in the period 1885–1890, before the welfare state, to 95 per 100,000 for the period 1905–1910, after much of the welfare state had been introduced. While these data do not directly test the hypothesis, they do suggest that the welfare state, far from having a suicide-pro-

ducing effect, appears to have reduced suicide in that segment of the population that benefited most from its provisions.

4. The suicide rate in the United States declined after the introduction of the social legislation of the New Deal. If we compare the pre-New Deal period 1925–1930 with the post-New Deal period of 1945–1950, avoiding the abnormal periods of the Depression and World War II, we find an average rate of about 13 per 100,000 in 1925–1930, compared with one of about 11 per 100,000 in 1945–1950.
5. The Canadian province of Saskatchewan, which has the most advanced welfare state provisions in Canada, has a suicide rate somewhat lower than that of the neighboring provinces. (The rate for males in Saskatchewan is 14.4 per 100,000; for Manitoba, 18.8; and for Alberta, 15.6.)

If we leave the level of statistical analysis and focus upon the more proximal psychological variables postulated by the welfare state-suicide hypothesis, the following facts emerge:

6. It has been maintained that the welfare state reduces incentive and thus fosters suicide. Sweden (presumably the country referred to by former President Eisenhower) is often viewed as the welfare state *par excellence*. Yet studies of Sweden reveal that the Swedes are characterized by a *high* degree of incentive, throwing themselves into their jobs with perhaps a greater intensity than do Americans.
7. In my own intensive interviews with suicide attempters in Norway and Denmark, I never encountered a case in which lack of incentive or boredom played a significant role. Nor have other investigators who have studied the motives of suicides in welfare states found these factors to be of any importance. Actually, boredom does not play a significant role in suicide in general. Cases of people so bored that they do not care to go on living are probably more frequent in novels than in real life. Such cases are psychopathological and do not involve, in the main, responses to the outside world.

Another piece of evidence is relevant: The questionnaire reveals that Norwegians are more bored with life than are

Danes. Since, it will be recalled, the Danish suicide rate is much higher than the Norwegian, it would appear highly unlikely that boredom can be linked with suicide.

8. The questionnaire findings reveal that the Norwegians possess stronger incentives toward success than do the Danes. Since both countries are welfare states, it would appear again, as in the case of Sweden, that welfare statism need not be associated with low incentive.
9. Are people in the welfare states, their moral fiber weakened by coddling, or their adaptation level lowered, less able to tolerate life's difficulties, as the hypothesis maintains? I could uncover no evidence to support this assertion. In my intensive interviews the reasons that emerged for the suicide attempts were the same kinds of reasons that are reported in non-welfare states. They were not, basically, trivial reasons. People do not lightly take their lives, either in welfare or non-welfare states.

As pointed out earlier, suicides in general tend to possess damaged personalities which render them less capable than normals of tolerating certain interpersonal frustrations. There is no evidence, however, that the welfare state produces such damage. My questionaire material suggests that there are proportionally more of these damaged personality types in Denmark than in Norway, although both are welfare states. This would hardly support the notion that it is the welfare state that produces personalities intolerant of frustration.

This, then is the evidence directly relating to the hypothesis. In each of nine tests the hypothesis is rejected.

If the belief is wrong, how does it come to attain such currency? There is, of course, the wishfulness of political conservatives. But there is also the fact that since a number of welfare states do have high suicide rates, it is easy to fall into the fallacy of assuming a causal linkage. It must be kept in mind however, that in these states, as in non-welfare states, there are also such developments as increased industrialization, technological change, urbanization, changes in work activities, new relations in marriage, changes in child-rearing practices, and many other factors that may well influence suicide rates.

If the welfare state does not cause suicide, then what, if any, relation exists between the two? We have already seen that in several instances the adoption of social welfare programs was followed by some decrease in suicide rates. It would seem that the reverse of the hypothesis may well be true: That the welfare state has at least a mildly ameliorative effect of reducing suicide.

There are two theoretical principles to support this position. First, suicide is a consequence of experienced deprivation; the welfare state does not deprive, but, on the contrary, supplies. It may supply little of what the potential suicide really needs, for his needs are, in the main, emotional ones in his personal life; but it supplies something. I have never, incidentally, encountered a man who attempted suicide because he had just received a social security check.

Second, the welfare state provides hopeful future outlooks. A man can look forward to an economically carefree retirement, unmarred by anxieties about the expenses of illness or disablement. Such a favorable future time-perspective is an antidote to suicide.

Yet these effects are not major. The welfare state mildly reduces suicide for a society as a whole; although, for disadvantaged groups within the society, the beneficial effects on the suicide rates are marked. Surely suicide is not increased by the welfare state.

Suicide and Civilization

What can be said of the relation between suicide and civilization? Is suicide one of civilization's discontents? Can we expect an increase in suicide as civilization spreads and matures?

The term "civilization" is not, of course, a precise concept. It is, moreover, difficult to define without being ethnocentric. For present purposes we shall think of it rather arbitrarily as characterized by such developments as industrialization, advanced technology, urbanization, complex bureaucratic development, and highly developed education. Much of the world is in fact moving in this direction. From the point of view of the present theory these are distal variables with complex and obscure relations to suicide.

A survey of countries and areas, with rough estimates of their level of civilization, fails to suggest any strong positive relationship between suicide and civilization. Some preliterate societies are reported to have very low suicide rates, others very high ones. In Europe, "highly civilized" Holland has a low rate; so does "less civilized" Spain. "Civilized" England and the United States have moderate rates. Perhaps some positive relation exists; but it can hardly be high, and it appears to present no easily explicable pattern.

One line of evidence is the historical: If the development of civilization is productive of suicide, one would expect rising rates as civilization advanced in many countries. Denmark, one of the few countries with relatively reliable statistics for the last one hundred years, does not reveal any marked rise over this period. The United States rate is about the same today as it was in 1900. This would seem to constitute strong evidence against any significant relationship between advancing civilization and suicide.

It seems fair to say that there is no fixed or necessary connection between civilization and suicide, that the relations that develop will depend upon specific developments within "civilization."

One possible development is a reduction in the amount of succorance available. Increased fractionization of society into small family groups lacking primary group support may, in accordance with our theory, result in increased suicide rates. However, the development of succorant social institutions could provide countereffects. It is difficult, at this point, to peer into the future and assess these possible trends.

Another possible development, already to be seen to some extent in an advanced country like Denmark, is the movement of mothers into the labor force, with work continuing through the child-bearing years with resultant maternal deprivation of infants and young children. This trend may be encouraged by feminist movements bent upon freeing women from the "burdens of motherhood." Such a development, in its production of a high proportion of psychologically damaged personalities, vulnerable to certain stresses, would lead to increased suicide rates. One cannot totally preclude the possibility that some day adequate substitutes for maternal care may be developed that do not result in damage to children. The danger is, however, that the general withdrawal of maternal care will take place long before any such possible advances. Countries under pressure to expand production rapidly are particularly prone to encroach upon the child-rearing process.

Another danger is that revolutionary states may introduce early separation of children from mothers, so that the children can be indoctrinated ideologically and politically in the new values.

One possibly increasing need of civilization, as it becomes more complexly organized and bureaucratized, is for increasingly non-aggressive behavior in its citizens. Our analysis of the psychodynamics of suicide has not postulated the bridling of aggression as a direct cause of suicide but rather has suggested that difficulty in the control of aggression is characteristic of the kinds of personalities that are susceptible to suicide. That is, the same kind of damage early in life produces both difficulty in expressing aggression *and* the susceptibility to despair. But, to an extent, societies tend to produce the kind of people they need, somehow adjusting child rearing to meet these needs. (Erich Fromm has made this observation, as has, more sophisticatedly, Erik Erikson.) If, then, highly civilized societies will need unaggressive people, they may well produce them by the very same methods that produce the suicidally susceptible. Such a development, then, could lead to an increase in future suicide rates.

In summing up, it seems clear that no confident prediction can be made about suicide and the future development of civilization. Civilization is no unitary development: It contains trends and countertrends and their directions lie in the murky future. Some possible trends appear to be productive of suicide, others not. It must not be forgotten that increased knowledge may allow us to avoid current pathogenic practices. Surely the evidence does not allow us to assert, as is often done, that the development of civilization will lead to mounting suicide rates.

7

Toward a General Theory

Science attempts to develop general statements that indicate the conditions under which an event will occur, that is, statements of the form: if . . . ., then . . . . The selection of the terms for denoting these conditions, the appropriate concepts, from all the great welter of phenomena and possible abstractions from phenomena, constitutes probably the most difficult of the tasks of science. To be successful, these concepts need to be selected from precisely the right locus in nature and to be at precisely the right level of abstraction. Moreover, one of the qualities of this optimal level of abstraction in the formulation of a general theory in the social sciences must be that the concepts will be applicable both cross-culturally and to different historical periods. Finally, the successful theory must indicate the structural relationships among the concepts, the manner in which they fit together.

In the social sciences these demands may be impossible to meet, for it is far from certain that stable natural systems exist in the social world that are amenable to the relatively neat formulations possible for the physical universe.

The present theory has striven to be guided as much as was feasible by the requirements listed above. It has perhaps met some of them, but it clearly remains incomplete. For example, the conditional variables, particularly on the sociological level, may bear structural relations to each other that are not indicated.

In the construction of the present theory, the initial broad formula indicates the locus and kinds of variables involved:

$$(1) \qquad S = f\,(V, D)$$

stating that the Probability of Suicide is a function of a Vulnerability in the Personality and the degree of certain Deprivations. A basic model that takes into account both personality and situational factors and conceives the behavior in question as the outcome of an interaction between the two is probably applicable not only to suicide but to a broad range of psychological and sociological problems. Although such a model may seem a truism, and indeed lip service is often paid to it, its implications have not usually been seriously considered in theory construction.

It is further maintained that the basic, proximal variable most sensitively related to suicide is Hope, to which it is inversely related:

$$(2) \qquad S = f\left(\frac{1}{H}\right)$$

Hope itself, however, represents the outcome of the interaction between a basic personality variable, the Sense of Competence (C) and an input variable, a Threat to acceptable life conditions (T).

$$(3) \qquad H = f\left(\frac{C}{T}\right)$$

$$\text{and } (4) \qquad S = f\left(\frac{T}{C}\right)$$

which is a more specific rendering of equation (1). *This may be seen as the basic proximal equation for the conditions of suicide.* Its variables, perforce, are psychological.

The variable called D in the broad equation (1) and T in the more specific equation (4) may be expanded distally into the *social surround* in terms of various social influences that have a relatively direct bearing upon it, and, therefore, upon suicide. Thus:

$$(5) \qquad S = f\left(\frac{DEC,\ DIG,\ TS}{Su,\ HFT}\right)$$

in which:
S = Probability of Suicide
DEC = Demands for the Exercising of Competence
DIG = Demands for Interpersonal Giving
TS = Tolerance of Suicide
Su = Availability of Succorance
HFT = Degree of Hope in the Future Time Perspective of the Society.

This may be seen as the basic equation for denoting the variables in the social surround related to suicide. It encompasses, I believe, the major proximal social variables that are relatively powerful in determining suicide rates.

If now we reformulate into social terms the variable of Vulnerability (V) in equation (1) as the frequency of Production of Personalities Injured in their Sense of Competence (PIC), and combine it with Equation (5), we obtain:

$$(6) \qquad S = f\left(\frac{PIC,\ DEC,\ DIG,\ TS}{Su,\ HFT}\right)$$

This may be seen as the basic proximal sociological equation for suicide.

These equations are simple mathematicizations; they are clearly not quantifications. The question of the extent to which we can validly quantify in psychology and sociology is still, I believe, an open one. There is of course an enormous amount of quantification in these sciences and much of it, as in demography, is obviously useful. There is also, unfortunately, much trivial, misleading, and pretentious quantification which suggests a degree of precision and relevance that is in fact lacking. A strong case can be made, I believe, for the position that these sciences will never achieve the kind of quantitative precision possible in the physical sciences.

Yet we should attempt to move in the direction of quantification, even if it must be crude. It should not prove insurmountably difficult, for example, to develop scales for the psychological equations of the degree of Hope and perhaps of the Threat to acceptable life conditions, and the Sense of Competence itself. Broad ratings, such as High, Medium, and Low might at first be used, with appropriate numbers assigned to each. Similarly, on the societal level, broad ratings might be developed for each of the variables in Equation (6) and the equations assayed cross-culturally. Only then might it be possible to introduce mathematical constants into the equations and to apply relative weights to the variables.

The Suicidal Society

There is a curious theoretical relationship that must now be noted. It is perhaps best approached by entering the seamless web of culture at the point of the production by certain child-rearing practices of a high proportion of individuals wounded in their sense of competence and therefore psychologically dependent. These people, we have suggested, are more vulnerable, under certain stresses, to suicide. This is, for the individual, the basic model.

However, if we now look at a population containing a large proportion of such individuals in its role of *constituting the social surround* for its members, new influences emerge. An individual is surrounded by and interacts with others who suffer from the same wounds as himself. And what are the symptoms of these wounds? First, it will be recalled, there is an insatiable craving for succorance. Consequently, there will be in this culture many people making insatiable demands for succorance upon each other.

Secondly, these are people who often have difficulty in giving, especially of succorance. Themselves feeling weak, incompetent, and deprived, they can hardly themselves give. We are thus confronted with the situation of the *psychologically hungry demanding of those who cannot give.*

The hungry are frustrated, enraged, thrown into despair. They face a social environment that not only fails to give to them but is rendered intolerably difficult by clamoring to take from them.

Further, these people are oversensitive to any indication of rejection and abandonment, for that was the nature of their original wound. But rejection is precisely what they encounter as they make their demands upon those who can least meet them. Again, there is rage in the frustrated and rage in the frustrators for the unjust accusations and resentments against them.

Thus there is rage, some repressed, some expressed, all producing rejection and abandonment for those who can least tolerate it. Friends and loved ones are alienated, resulting in isolation and loneliness. Analysts who stress isolation and loneliness as primary causes of suicide often fail to see the processes of which these are but end products.

We have, thus, a system of vicious cycles. A society consisting of many such psychologically disturbed people becomes, then, a sick society. To be sure, we must remind ourselves that even such societies contain psychologically healthy people and many only slightly wounded, as well as stabilizing social institutions, so that the society can function on the whole rather successfully. But it is apt to have, along with other problems, high suicide rates.

From a theoretical point of view it will be seen that there is something of a departure here from the usual structure of social thought. Much attention has been focused upon the influence of society and culture upon personality. Indeed, in European social thought, this direction of causality has been just about the exclusive one. Here the reverse direction is focused upon, that of personality upon society. More precisely, a theoretical point of view is required, according to which *individual personalities are perceived as responders to society and at the same time as constituting the social surround, that is, society itself.* Moreover, both of these influences must be perceived simultaneously. What is special in the present analysis is that the same defect in personality that is directly involved in the suicidal breakdown is also, in another facet and in another person, responsible as social agent for the breakdown. That is, the higher the proportion of the vulnerable in a society, the greater the probability that they will encounter and interact with suicide-producing others; that is, people like themselves. The degree to which a society produces this personality type, *both vulnerable and wounding*, thus becomes a central issue.

It becomes evident that the personality factor in suicide, by playing a dual role, is more powerfully involved than might have been suspected. One might assert, perhaps, borrowing from another discipline, that there is a kind of Keynesian multiplier effect, with a given increase in the number of vulnerable personalities in a society resulting in disproportionately large numbers of suicides.

This theoretical point requires elaboration. It is clear that the variable Availability of Succorance is not independent of the personality variable, the Vulnerability factor, but rather is to an extent an inverse function of it. That is, the vulnerable, low in their sense of competence, are often unable to give succorance, thus presenting, in their role of those responded to, a cold and rejecting social environment.

More formally stated:

$$\text{(7)} \qquad Su = f\left(\frac{1}{V_1}\right) = f\,(C_1)$$

In which Su is the Availability of Succorance in a society, V is the frequency of individuals in that society suffering from the particular vulnerability, and C the average level of the Sense of Competence among individuals in that society.

The Prediction of Suicide

Valid laws, it is often said, should be able to predict. However —and there appears to exist considerable confusion—they cannot predict into an unknown future. They are, it will be recalled, statements of the form of: if........, then......... They can predict, for either individuals or groups, only if the conditions at the time for which the prediction is made are known. The equations of the theory presented here are all ahistorical; they consist of conditions known to exist in the field at a given time and an outcome at that time. If we can assume with confidence that certain conditions will exist in the future, then we can employ the equations as predictors.

Conditional predictions are thus possible. We can predict from Equation (2) that if a given individual ever finds himself in a condition of extremely low hope, then there is a high probability that he will commit suicide. So, too, if in a given society a certain condition is to be introduced, such as a decrease in the Availability of Succorance, then we might predict an increase in the suicide rate. We may not be able to predict with certainty that the *conditions* will occur, or if they do, just when.

There are yet other circumstances in which we can predict. When we are reasonably certain that a present set of conditions will continue into the future, then we are in the position of knowing the future conditions and we can apply our equations for that time. Thus, if we make the plausible assumption that the low state of hope in which the person now finds himself is apt to continue at least for a while, we can predict that the probability of his committing suicide in the near future is, according to our Equation (2), high.

So, too, Equation (4), which treats of the components of hope, can accomplish a certain degree of prediction. The basic sense of competence, once established early in life, may not change readily. Therefore, on the basis of an appraisal made at the present time of a low sense of competence in an individual, we can predict that the probabilities of his committing suicide at some time are relatively high. Further, if we can assume, for example, that his seriously ailing wife—upon whom his sense of competence depends—is apt to die soon, then we can predict his suicide with a much greater degree of confidence. This represents a high value of T in Equation (4).

The close linkage of Hope with the probability of suicide may have useful practical consequences. It may well be that the best short-term predictor of suicide is an estimate of the individual's hope. Thus a short standard interview or test might well be devised for assessing Hope at a particular time and used routinely in assessing suicide potential.

It has long been recognized that a history of suicide attempts by an individual is a rather strong predictor of eventual suicide. From the viewpoint of the present theory, this suggests a chronically low

Sense of Competence in that individual, who, whenever confronted with a strong Threat to acceptable life conditions, reacts with suicidal behavior. Previous suicidal behavior remains a powerful predictor.

On a sociological level, it will be recalled, for the prediction of suicide rates in countries or societies, the relevant formula is:

$$S = f\left(\frac{PIC,\ DEC,\ DIG,\ TS}{Su,\ HFT}\right) \tag{6}$$

These variables may perhaps initially be quantified by rough ratings on each of them for a given society in the categories High, Moderate, and Low, with appropriate numbers assigned to each. We may at this point lack data for most of these variables, but they are not in principle unmeasurable. Prediction from more distal variables is apt to be, for reasons we have already discussed, feeble and unstable.

Strategy for Theory Construction

The mode of analysis and theory construction employed here on the problem of suicide would seem to have broader application in the social sciences. Its characteristics may be summarized as follows:

1. The analysis is field theoretical, that is, it is ahistorical, seeking the forces determining an event at a particular time.
2. A two-factor interactive model involving personality factors and external forces is employed.
3. The forces, or variables, that are sought are those most proximal to the event, those perhaps belonging to the same "natural" system as the event. These will be psychological in character.
4. Slightly more distal influences may be sought by cautious extension from the proximal ones. These are apt to be social psychological variables. Sociological variables that are quite distal from the event tend to have feeble and unstable relations to the event and are therefore often of secondary scientific interest.

5. A simple mathematization is useful. The degree of quantification that is possible must remain as yet an open question.

6. Personality factors are seen in a dual role, both as actors and as constituting a social surround. A given increase in the frequency of a particular personality type in a society may thus produce a multiplier effect.

8

Social Engineering and Suicide Prevention

A viable theory of a disease should be able to generate suggestions concerning the prevention of it. True, one may not have in one's hands the levers to effect the cure, but one should at least be able to indicate where the levers are located. Fortunately, however, with respect to suicide there are some levers that are accessible.

Since culture is indeed something of a "seamless web," difficult to enter and not easily amenable to manipulation of its strands or predictable with regard to the effects of an introduced change, any suggestions concerning deliberate social engineering must be made with caution. It has become rather chic to point to such difficulties as a reason for avoiding the prickly problem of social engineering, but the difficulties are not in fact insurmountable and the serious theorist must attempt to engage them.

What suggestions, then, does our theory of suicide generate? Basically, and most broadly, it follows from the theory that greater degrees of hope be somehow developed in man's life outlook.

It will be recalled that hope is a function of both personality and external conditions. The raising of the level of hope, therefore, should attempt intervention in both realms.

It follows from the general theory:

$$S = f\left(\frac{\text{Threat to Acceptable Life Conditions}}{\text{Sense of Competence}}\right) = f\left(\frac{1}{\text{Hope}}\right)$$

that to lower the value of S, the severity of the Threat should be diminished and the Sense of Competence enhanced, thus raising the level of Hope and lowering the probability of Suicide.

It will be recalled that the theory asserted that with regard to the production of personalities damaged in their sense of competence in a given society there operated a kind of Multiplier Effect, with such individuals acting both as responders and as those responded to, so that a given increase in such individuals would have relatively large effects upon the society's suicide rate. So, too, a decrease in the production of such personalities would have a Divisor Effect, with a decrease both in the number of the vulnerable and in the number of the rejecting and ungiving with whom they interact.

With regard, first, to these roots of hope in the personality, we must move toward the production of fewer people whose ability to sustain hope is vulnerable and fragile. More positively, we must raise children with a strong, resilient sense of competence to carry into adult life.

We have seen that our present knowledge of the nature of the wounding in infancy and childhood that leads to adult personalities that are later vulnerable is not definitive. We are not certain as to what developmental stages in infancy and childhood are the most vulnerable and in exactly what way. But the evidence is strong that maternal deprivation, prolonged abandonment, sensory deprivation, or absence of "mothering," can result in a failure of the infant and young child to develop a basic sense of trust in the environment, thus disturbing the development of a sense of competence and the erection of a resilient sense of hope upon it.

There is little doubt that deprivations of this type contribute to the function of various other mental disorders as well, including psychoses. As already suggested, the precise constellations of infant treatment, the developmental phase of the infant or young child at which the insult occurs, and the innate temperamental factors that tend to produce one mental disorder rather than another are not yet well understood. We do not know precisely which tends to produce those most vulnerable to suicide, but it is abundantly clear that there is everything to be gained from avoiding exposure of the young to any of the various psychic insults that appear to be the agents.

Child care specialists have in recent years tended to advise strongly avoidance of these insults, but one continues to encounter many instances of gross and tragic violations of this advice. Sometimes through the grinding circumstances of poverty, sometimes through ignorance, sometimes through the psychological difficulties of the parents, infants are still abandoned for long periods and otherwise maltreated. To counteract such maltreatment, society must bring to bear all the weight of its great resources, including intensified educational efforts through the mass media, the focusing of the attention of social workers on prevention, and the strengthening of laws against this kind of maltreatment of infants and young children.

Infants and young children in institutions such as foundling homes, nurseries, and orphanages can be mass victims. The search for substitutes for such mass handling should be intensified, as in adoption and foster-home plans, and, where such institutions are unavoidable, staffs should be sufficiently large and well trained to provide adequate "mothering."

The sudden and psychologically unprepared separation of young children from mothers through hospitalization of the child, which can be traumatic, can also be mitigated by education of mothers and hospital staffs, and by having the mother present as much as is feasible during the child's hospital stay. Children should also be psychologically prepared for a hospital stay.

Although it appears that the earliest bases of trust, sense of competence, and hope are laid down in infancy, there is good reason to believe, as we have seen, that later influences are important. Methods of rearing children beyond infancy should both avoid attacks upon the sense of competence and attempt positively to reinforce it. "Conditional love" on the part of the parents for the child—"If you fail in school, mother won't love you anymore"—in which the prospect of failure is accompanied by the terror of abandonment, must be avoided. Attempts by the child to master his environment, both physical and social, should be encouraged, his successes applauded. Above all, devaluation, so directly destructive of the sense of competence, should be avoided.

The identity that emerges in children during the early school years, when the sense of competence is enlarged and made more conscious, can benefit from encouragement and the demonstration of mastery over tasks. The construction of graded challenges, custom tailored for each child, which can be met and conquered, may be salutory.

There seems little doubt that the earliest wounds to the personality are inflicted in the malfunctioning of the symbiotic relationship between infant and mother. But, as we have seen, fathers play an important role in the development of the sense of competence. They can avoid intimidation of the child, with its destructive effects upon the sense of competence and its tendency, it would seem, to produce an anxiety-laden compulsive identification with them. They can provide a model that exemplifies a healthy male's sense of competence. They can avoid that curiously pathological disparagement of children that is prevalent in some groups. They can positively encourage the gropings toward mastery of the environment that is normally manifested in children.

So too during adolescence, with its reactivation of earlier conflicts and its hunt for identity, is the sense of competence often in peril. If this is recognized and more widely appreciated, perhaps more direct and positive ways can be developed for stabilizing the wobbling sense of competence that plagues adolescence.

Among adults, a damaged sense of competence is not easily repaired. Psychotherapy has probably helped some, but repairing severe early damage via existing techniques has not proved to be one of the great areas of success of modern psychotherapy. It may be that bold departures in psychotherapy are both necessary and possible, that more direct methods may be developed of repairing a damaged sense of competence than now exist among the tired current psychotherapies.

Psychotherapy with suicidal patients represents special difficulties and hazards. Such patients may be extremely dependent and demanding of the therapist, as well as, on occasion, unpleasantly aggressive. The therapist, despite his professional posture, may well develop hostile feelings in his countertransference toward the patient, leading to some kind of rejection of the patient. But this is precisely where the patient is most vulnerable, and suicide often results. Therapists should be acutely aware of the danger of this development so that they may bend all efforts to counteract it.

Recently, McClelland and his associates have reported dramatic success in training adults to higher levels of the achievement motive with consequent marked behavioral changes. There would appear to be some relation between this motive and the sense of competence; but the evidence suggests that what McClelland has been training is mainly certain techniques such as risk taking, for example, rather than more basic psychological processes. Such successes, limited as they may be, suggest that bold an imaginative experimentation in this area may not prove fruitless.

A problem that requires close examination is that of working mothers. In advanced countries, a whole complex of developments has contributed to a sharp increase in the number of working married women. Among these developments are the increased education of women, the reduction in the demands of housekeeping, increased availability of jobs, increase in jobs not requiring physical strength, the desirability of increased family income, and the breakdown in prejudice against women. Barring major economic reversals, the proportion of working married women is likely to increase. To be sure, some of these women are childless or have grown children, but some enter the job market while their offspring are still infants or young children. The arrangements made for care of these young in the mothers' absence, involving baby-sitters and nurseries, are frequently unsatisfactory for the children's mental health.

It is not possible to be dogmatic about working mothers of infants and young children; individual situations may differ. But it is perhaps fair to suggest that mothers of infants and young children avoid taking outside employment except under exceptional pressures and circumstances. The risks are too great.

There is yet another possible development to which advanced countries may become increasingly susceptible. This is the seductive idea that infants and children could be much more efficiently brought up in groups away from their mothers and families. Political leaders may be attracted by the prospect of freeing the mothers to augment the labor force as well as by the possibility of indoctrinating future citizens with values that the state itself most highly regards. Such policies are not necessarily linked to any particular ideology and may emerge in a broad political spectrum of states eager to rationalize their economies under a uniform ideology. It should be clear, however, that great dangers lurk in such developments.

Societies might well avoid institutionalized possibilities of acute attacks upon the sense of competence. For example, in Japan many suicides are reported to occur when youths take the crucial examinations which determine their entire future lives. Failure, and fear of failure, have shattering effects on the sense of competence and on hope among Japanese youths. So too might the somewhat inadequate social security system, with its destructive effects on the middle-aged, be reformed.

Thus far, we have been concerned mainly with actions to be avoided. The more difficult problem, undoubtedly, is the recommendation of positive actions against suicide. There are changes that might indeed be helpful but are impracticable: for example, to urge people in general to love each other more and supply help and support to the desperate. Indeed, it is quite possible that our increasingly technological society will move even further away from a conditions of close affectional ties among individuals.

Unemployment is a social ill that is acutely destructive of the sense of competence. Indeed, among demographic variables, unemployment shows one of the highest correlations with suicide rates. In addition to the economic waste and the misery derived from unemployment, this evil should be mitigated also for its production of suicides.

Since the repression and inhibition of aggression are involved in the psychodynamics of suicide, there is always the temptation to seek as a solution legitimate and noninjurious outlets for aggression. Our analysis suggests, however, that there is no promising solution to be found along these lines. Difficulties in the easy expression of aggression represent an intermediate process in the suicide-prone; behind these difficulties lies the tremendous ambivalence of love and hate toward someone very close. They could hardly be urged to aggress against these people—who are apt to be wives, husbands, or mothers—and aggression against other objects is largely irrelevant. We are not dealing with generalized aggression that only needs siphoning off; urging an abandoned wife to punch the pillows will hardly prove effective. Such acts have no fundamental effect upon the sense of competence. We come back to the more basic recommendation: The society must produce more of the *kinds of personalities*, secure in their sense of competence who, among other things, dare to express aggression.

On a social level, one possibility may be tentatively considered. In societies that are restrictive of both sex and aggression, some periodic institutionalized indulgence could act to reduce pent-up tension and a sense of deprivation. The Roman Saturnalia might have had some desirable effects. In our culture, the institution of "Saturday night" among lower-class Negroes, with its indulgence in drinking, sex, and fighting may be psychologically helpful and indeed may contribute somewhat to the lowness of the Negro suicide rate. On the other hand, the socially undesirable aspects of "Saturday night" hardly recommend it as an institution to be fostered.

Our society in general does have New Year's Eve, which involves some removal of customary barriers and to a lesser degree perhaps, the office Christmas party. That the extension of such institutions, even if it were quite feasible, would have any important effects upon suicide rates, however, seems dubious.

The situation of the Negro group, incidentally, may supply some clues to suicide prevention. The low suicide rate for Negroes is surprising in view of the fact that most of them belong to the lower socio-economic classes, which have a relatively high rate. One must note, however, that the very low Negro rates are most marked in the rural South and that in Northern cities the Negro rates are somewhat higher. Two of the variables in our theory would lead one to expect high Negro rates: the low level for them of hope in the future time-perspective of the society and the low level of the availability of succorance. On the other hand, demands for the exercising of competence are probably low, exerting an influence toward a low rate.

It is difficult to make any estimate concerning the production of personalities injured in their sense of competence in the Negro group. There could be something in Negro early child-rearing that lays down a strong basic sense of competence that later resists suicide. Alternatively, it may be that the kinds of early psychic wounds that Negroes receive predispose them toward certain psychopathologies, such as schizophrenia, rather than suicide. The problem is a complex one. One clue that emerges here is the possibility that low demands for the exercising of competence exert great weight in ameliorating suicidal pressures. Perhaps such demands are almost inevitable in modern society, but if they can be proved to be suicide-producing, our ingenuity should be turned toward softening their impact.

We have seen from our earlier analysis that the welfare state, far from being a cause of suicide as some have maintained, would appear to exert at least a mildly preventive influence. Suicides of the aged and infirm, precipitated by grinding poverty and economic helplessness, are clearly reduced by the provisions of the welfare state. But the overall influence of the welfare state upon suicide is only marginal, and the movement toward the welfare state in many advanced countries cannot be expected to have any major effects on suicide rates. Nonetheless, from the viewpoint of suicide prevention at least, the welfare state should be encouraged.

The most daring feats of social engineering are those involving the injection of new values into a culture. Such feats are perhaps impossible if the culture is not "ready" for such values, that is, if no existing needs can be engaged and intractable social structures exist. In the case of suicide, following our basic formula, the infusion of values rich in hope could well act to reduce suicide rates. We have seen that the achievement of high hope is dependent partly upon a deep-seated personality component, the sense of competence, and partly upon a component present in the outside world. Quite possibly it is this outer component that is the more easily manipulable. Activities expressing values that we hold dear and external events that profoundly influence our lives can, if they involve favorable expectations, have considerable effect in raising the level of hope.

Thus, in underdeveloped countries, citizens who have thrown themselves into the task of building up their country, if they feel that the future outlook for their task is hopeful, are highly immunized against suicide. Such persons are reported to possess an élan that is rare elsewhere.

We have seen earlier that the space of free movement, which is closely related to hope, becomes highly constricted in suicide. It follows that opening it up would be antisuicidal. Open societies, then, rich in opportunities both for economic and self-fulfillment, presenting ideals for which men strive, can only be beneficial. And we must not forget that the space of free movement is also dependent upon inner resources which may be engaged. It is significant that in the horrors of the concentration camps some survived because they opened and entered areas in their inner space of free movement, hopes to which they staunchly clung.

But what, in technologically more mature countries, could be the equivalent of such generators of hope? The established religions provide hope for some, but in the main they no longer engage the emotions sufficiently deeply to provide a nourishing antisuicidal hope. Nor are there new religions on the horizon that could be bearers of hope. Conceptions like that of "The Great Society," although they contain elements of the political slogan, also involve programs of true grandeur which might possibly—just possibly—engage the hopes of many. Perhaps in the purification and beautification of man's environment, in the quest for social justice, hopeful commitment for man can be found. Thus far, except for a handful of individuals, these values have not succeeded in capturing the emotions. Possibly energetic campaigns, integrated with the schools and the churches, could begin to encourage the growth of such values. A nation hopefully engaged is not a nation of high suicide rates.

The interrelations between the contributions of personality and of social factors are extremely complex, for, among other problems, these represent different levels of abstraction. Moreover, there is, through time, a kind of special relation between them, with personality factors influencing the forms of society and society contributing to the molding of personality.

Much has been written about the existence of alienation in our society, of the tendency of many individuals to reject their culture, not to feel themselves to be part of it. There is, one suspects, considerable overlap between the alienated and the suicidal states and not totally dissimilar causal factors in the personality and in society. The mistrust of other people, the pessimism, tend to be common to both suicide and alienation. But alienation may also be a way station to suicide in that the victim perceives himself as receiving no love or support from his society, but only cold rejection.

From the point of view of suicide prevention, it would appear desirable to reduce those forces that produce alienation. Unfortunately, it is far from clear as to what exactly in our swiftly changing technological society contributes to individual alienation. However, the general principle remains valid, that suicide will be reduced by the introduction into society of sources of hope, of institutions that foster the sense of competence, that supply something of succorance and even love. Hope may well be ignited among the activist elements of a promising underdeveloped country, but the problem is more complex in a wealthy society in which material possessions do not, for many, generate soaring hopes.

Behind the feeling of hope lies the sense of competence. The main foundation of this sense is laid down early in life. Nonetheless, this basic feeling, though not easily changed, can be either enhanced or diminished by significant experiences and conditions.

The deliberate management of the sense of competence on a societal level can only be the subject of cautious speculation. In principle one can conceive, on the one hand, of societies that make its individual members feel powerless, and, on the other, societies that might support and even enhance the individual's confidence about his abilities and his place in society. Possibly during the process of education a sense of the importance of the individual's role in his society can be communicated. Possibly greater individual participation in the decision processes can be of help in vast impersonal industries. More basically, however, one has the impression that the entire psychic cement of a society is involved, and that minor adjustments can have but minor effects.

Another long-range cultural possibility is the broadening of the number of life styles and performances that might be labeled as successful. At present in the West, mainly material success and certain visible achievements are labeled as "success," and many who fail to achieve these experience failure and an attack upon their sense of competence. Perhaps merely *being* an excellent person, benevolent or witty or wise, without spectacular achievements should also be viewed as successful.

The problem of the sinking into despair of the aged with subsequent suicide is a complex one. In cases in which incurable or unbearably painful illnesses are involved, the remedies—for what they are worth—are obvious. Where the aged are harrassed by poverty, the development of social services and the welfare state has in recent years brought alleviation.

But despair in old age also has less acute causes. The existential fact of the decline of one's powers and the inevitable imminence of death can hardly fail to attack the fabric of hope. Those with personality structures built upon a strong base of early trust and hope will perhaps best be able to ward off this despair. Over the longer term it may be possible to develop attitudes toward death in our culture which can face and accept it more fully, supplanting our contemporary attempt at avoidance of any thought of it.

Further, and again over the long term, it may be possible to develop in our society a more honorable and useful role for the elderly, a status that does not leave them feeling rejected and superfluous, wounded in their sense of competence.

Some effect upon suicide rates might also be expected from medical advances against diseases now considered hopeless, since a sizable proportion of suicides take place upon discovery that one is suffering from a hopeless disease. Similarly, medical advances against prolonged pain associated with various diseases should act to mitigate intolerable situations.

There is one social stress noted in the theory that is perhaps somewhat amenable to manipulation. That is the great demands placed on people occupying certain roles and occupations in our society. Certain executives, some physicians, perhaps some sales personnel are subjected to great demands, often interpersonal ones. They must "give" of themselves to others to a degree they may find intolerable. While not a predominant cause of suicide, these stresses may contribute. At this point it is difficult to say what effects a computerized technology will have upon these stresses. It may ease the burdens of many, while placing heavier ones upon a few. In any case, mitigation of these stresses by such devices as alleviation of heavy responsibility, the provision of assistants, frequent vacations, and so on, may be of some help.

Suicide Prevention Centers

People in desperation may contemplate suicide, but many are reluctant and conflicted about it. They may maintain bits of hope and they may emit cries for help. For such cases, the suicide prevention center can be of great value. For those whose hope is still sufficiently viable for them to communicate with a center, the point of no return toward suicide may never be reached if the center can intervene in time. Those adamantly bent upon suicide, whose spark of hope is well nigh extinguished, will not, of course, communicate with a center.

Thus there is a self-selection involved in the kind of people treated by suicide prevention centers, with the most severe cases precluding themselves. Yet, as we have seen, a much larger number of people are to be found in the conflicted, hesitant group than in the group adamantly determined upon suicide. The number of potential cases that might be treated by preventive centers is clearly enormous.

And yet, even among those cases not irrevocably bent upon suicide, the impulse to communicate with a prevention center may never manifest itself. The feeling that the difficulty is a private one that no outsider could do anything about may prevent communication with a prevention center. So too may be narrowing of attention that accompanies the depression preceding many suicides: Telephoning a center may never even occur to one in such a state. Perhaps, too, those who telephone are the more histrionic, the self-dramatizers, not the shy, not the alienated. Thus, even among those not irrevocably bent upon suicide, the proportion who might telephone might be considerably smaller than one might hope.

By its very nature the suicide prevention center can intervene only in the very late stages of the long process leading to suicide; people are apt to telephone only when they feel suicide might be imminent. Yet, since the motivational forces at such a point may be exquisitely balanced between life and death, the intervention can be crucial.

Treatment of suicidal cases in prevention centers must be based upon a rebuilding of hope and the sense of competence. Toward this end the dependent relationship of the potential victim to the therapist can be rapidly developed and used.

The balance may be tipped toward life by a perceptual widening of the patient's view of his problem, by the supplying of the succorance he craves, by practical help. Suicide prevention centers, therefore, while they may provide no basic remedy, represent an important social institution marshalled against suicide. The pioneering yet sophisticated work of the Suicide Prevention Center of Los Angeles and of other centers following in its footsteps reveals how valuable such institutions can be.

In the light of our general theory, the management and treatment of the suicidal and depressive in mental hospitals should be modified. Mental hospital staffs are extremely anxious to prevent suicide among patients and go to great lengths to prevent it by removing any possible objects that might be used as suicide weapons, by strict surveillance and sharp constriction of the patient's freedom in the institution. Indeed, as Goffman has pointed out, even the nonsuicidal patient is often deprived of his normal clothing and personal belongings.

In these ways, and in others more subtle, patients are often treated as if they are totally incompetent. *These blows, administered to a sense of competence already in something of a state of collapse, may well act to precipitate suicide.*

It follows, then, that while adequate precautions against suicide by patients in hospitals must be taken, every effort should also be bent toward avoiding unnecessary attacks upon their sense of competence and toward using every opportunity to strengthen it.

We have touched upon a number of possible approaches toward engineering a reduction in suicide. Some involve actions to be avoided, others actions to be taken. Some are short range, others long range. Some are practicable, others but faint possibilities. As with most social change, a broad multipronged attack mobilizing as many of the forces as possible stands the greatest chance of success.

Successful theories in the physical sciences may or may not have immediate practical application. In the social sciences and in psychology, a viable theory of social or individual pathology should, one might presume, supply at least the promise of cures for that ill. The present general theory generates and suggests a number of actions against suicide. Theory can have great power; we can be hopeful that the human scourge of suicide can, if not be vanquished, at least rendered a less considerable menace.

Appendix

A number of different types of observations and investigations were carried out:

1. An analysis of the epidemiology of suicide and the statistics of possibly related social variables, primarily of Norway and Denmark but also of other countries.

2. Observations of the social institutions and cultures of Norway and Denmark. Native informants were used in addition to direct observation. The methods, essentially ethnological, focused on a broad range of materials—from the national economy to folk tales and comic strips. Relevant historical material was also investigated.

Of particular interest was the attempt to uncover differences in child-rearing practices in the two countries that might relate to later suicidal behavior.

3. On the assumption that normal Norwegians and Danes would differ from each other in character structure and that clues to self-

destructive behavior and its absence might be found in such differences, a comparison was made of fairly large samples of Norwegians and Danes (180 in each country) by the use of questionnaires embodying personality and value items that were hypothesized as being related to suicide. The questionnaires were administered to university students in each country, based upon the methodological consideration that since these groups occupy comparable positions in the two countries, major social variables such as age, education and occupation are kept constant, so that differences found between them are in the main attributable to nationality. This is a methodological device that I devised and employed in my earlier studies of English and American personality structures. The full questionnaire used in the study included much material not directly relevant to suicide and therefore is not reproduced here.

4. A small number of intensive clinical interviews (about twenty in each country) was carried out in the hospitals of Oslo, Norway and Copenhagen, Denmark, with persons recovering from suicide attempts, with a view toward reconstructing the psychological and social conditions of the patient at the time of the attempt, the conditions leading to it, the social history, and some clues as to the psychodynamics of the attempt.

○

Bibliography

Adler, Alfred. *The Practice and Theory of Individual Psychology* (New York: Harcourt, Brace and World, 1929).

Andersen, Hans Christian. *Fairy Tales*. Edited by Svend Larsen, translated by R. P. Keigwin (Odense, Denmark: Flensted, 1960, 4 vols).

Arentsen, K., and Strømgren, E. "Patients in Danish Psychiatric Hospitals," *Acta Jutlandica, Medical Series* 9, Aarhus, Denmark, 1959.

Assael, Marcel I. "Thanatophilia," *Diseases of the Nervous System*, December, 1965, 777-781.

Block, Jeanne, and Christiansen, Bjørn, "A Test of Hendin's Hypotheses Relating Suicide to Child-Rearing Orientations," *Scandinavian Journal of Psychology*, 1967, 7, 267-288.

Bloom, Victor. An Analysis of Suicide at a Training Center, *American Journal of Psychiatry*, 1967, *123* (8) 918-925.

Boas, Louise Schutz. *Harriet Shelley, Five Long Years* (Fair Lawn, N.J.: Oxford University Press, 1962).

Bohannan, Paul, Ed. *African Homicide and Suicide* (Princeton: Princeton University Press, 1960).

Bowlby, John. "Grief and Mourning in Early Childhood," *The Psychoanalytic Study of the Child, 15,* 9-52 (New York: International Universities Press, 1960).

——. *Maternal Care and Mental Health.* Geneva: World Health Organization Monograph No. 2, 1951.

Casler, Lawrence. "Maternal Deprivation: A Critical Review of the Literature," *Monographs of the Society for Research in Child Development,* Serial No. 80, 1961, 26 (2).

Breed, Warren. "Occupational Mobility and Suicide," *American Sociological Review,* April, 1963, 28 (2) 179-188.

Cavan, Ruth S. *Suicide* (Chicago: University of Chicago Press, 1928).

Cohen, Elie A. *Human Behavior in the Concentration Camp* (New York: Grosset and Dunlap, 1953).

Connery, Donald. *The Scandinavians* (London: Eyre and Spottiswoode, 1966).

Coopersmith, Stanley. *The Antecedents of Self-Esteem* (San Francisco: W. H. Freeman, 1967).

Devereux, George. *Mohave Ethnopsychiatry and Suicide: The Psychiatric Knowledge and the Psychic Disturbances of an Indian Tribe* (Washington: Smithsonian Institution, Bureau of American Ethnology Bulletin 175, 1961).

DeVos, G. A. "Deviancy and Social Change: A Psychocultural Evaluation of Trends in Japanese Delinquency and Suicide," in Smith, R. J., and Beardsley, R. K., Eds. *Japanese Culture: Its Development and Characteristics* (Chicago: Aldine Publishing Co., 1962).

Douglas, Jack D. *The Social Meanings of Suicide* (Princeton, N.J.: Princeton University Press, 1967).

Dreyer, Karen. "Comparative Suicide Statistics," *Danish Medical Bulletin,* 1959 (6).

Dublin, Louis I. *Suicide: A Sociological and Statistical Study* (New York: The Ronald Press, 1963).

Durkheim, Emile. *Suicide: A Study in Sociology* (Glencoe, Ill.: The Free Press, 1951).

Eliot, Thomas D., Hilman, Arthur, et al. *Norway's Families* (Philadelphia: The University of Pennsylvania Press, 1960).

Erikson, Erik H., *Childhood and Society* (New York: W. W. Norton, 1963; second edition).

——. *Insight and Responsibility* (New York: W. W. Norton, 1964).

Ettlinger, Ruth, and Flordh, Per. "Attempted Suicide: Experience of Five Hundred Cases at a General Hospital," *Acta Psychiatrica et Neurologica Scandinavica,* Supplement 103, 4-45, Copenhagen, 1955.

Farber, M. L. "Time Perspective and Feeling Tone: A Study in the Perception of the Days," *Journal of Psychology,* 1953, 35, 253-257.

——. "Suffering and Time Perspective of the Prisoner," *University of Iowa Studies in Child Welfare,* 1944, 20, 155-227.

Farberow, N. L. "Personality Patterns of Suicidal Mental Patients," *Genetic Psychology Monographs,* 1950, 42, 3-79.

—— and Shneidman, E. S. *The Cry for Help* (New York: McGraw-Hill, 1961).

Feifel, Herman, Ed. *The Meaning of Death* (New York: McGraw-Hill, 1959).

Firth, Raymond. "Suicide and Risk-Taking in Tikopia Society," *Psychiatry,* 1961, *24* (1) 1-17.

Fremming, Kurt H. *The Expectation of Mental Infirmity in a Sample of the Danish Population* (London: The Eugenics Society and Cassell & Co., 1951).

Freud, Sigmund. *Civilization and its Discontents* (New York: W. W. Norton, 1962).

——. "Mourning and Melancholia," in *Collected Papers,* Vol. IV (London: The Hogarth Press, 1949).

——. "Homosexuality in a Woman," in *Collected Papers,* Vol. II (London: The Hogarth Press, 1949).

Fromm, Erich. *Man for Himself* (New York: Holt, Rinehart and Winston, 1947).

Gibbs, Jack P., and Martin, Walter T. "A Theory of Status Integration and Its Relation to Suicide," *American Sociological Review,* 1958, *23,* 140-147.

—— and Martin, Walter T. *Status Integration and Suicide* (Eugene, Oregon: The University of Oregon, 1964).

Goffman, E. *Asylums* (Garden City, N.Y.: Anchor Books, 1961).

Gordon, J. E. Lindemann, E., Ipsen, J., and Vaughan, W. T. "An Epidemiological Analysis of Suicide," in *Epidemiology of Mental Disorder* (New York: Milbank Memorial Fund, 1950).

Greer, S., Gunn, M. B., and Koller, K. M. "Aetiological Factors in Attempted Suicide," *British Medical Journal, 2,* 1352-1355, 1966.

Hamsun, Knut. *Growth of the Soil* (New York: Alfred A. Knopf, 1920).

——. *Hunger* (New York: Alfred A. Knopf, 1921).

Harlow, Harry F., and Harlow, Margaret Kuenne. "Social Deprivation in Monkeys," *Scientific American,* November, 1962, 2-10.

Hartelius, Hans. "Suicide in Sweden 1925-1950," *Acta Psychiatrica et Neurologica Scandinavica,* 32 (2) 1957.

Heinicke, C. M. *Some Antecedents and Correlates of Guilt and Fear in Young Boys,* unpublished doctoral dissertation, Department of Social Relations, Harvard University, 1953.

Hemingway, Ernest. *A Moveable Feast* (New York: Charles Scribner's Sons, 1964).

Hendin, Herbert. *Suicide and Scandinavia* (New York and London: Grune and Stratton, 1964).

Henry, Andrew F., and Short, James F., Jr. *Suicide and Homicide* (Glencoe, Ill.: Free Press, 1954).

Hetherington, E. Mavis. "A Developmental Study of the Effects of the Sex of the Dominant Parent on Sex-Role Preference, Identification and Imitation in Children," *Journal of Personality and Social Psychology*, 1965, 2, 2, 188-194.

Hirsch, J. "Demography and Suicide," Part I. *Mental Hygiene*, October, 1959, *43*, 516-525.

——. "Methods and Fashions of Suicide," Part II. *Mental Hygiene*, April, 1960, *44*, 3-11.

——. "Dynamics of Suicide," Part III. *Mental Hygiene*, April, 1960, *44* (2) 274 ff.

Hotchner, A. E. *Papa Hemingway* (New York: Random House, 1966).

Iga, Mamoru. "Relation of Suicide Attempt and Social Structure in Kamakura, Japan," *International Journal of Social Psychiatry*, 1966, *12* (3) 221-232.

Inkeles, Alex. "Sociology and Psychology," in *Psychology: A Study of a Science*, Sigmund Koch, Ed., Vol. 6, 317-387 (New York: McGraw-Hill, 1963).

Inoguchi, Rikihei, Nakajima, Tadashi, with Pineau, Roger. *The Divine Wind* (New York: Bantam Books, 1960).

Keniston, Kenneth. *The Uncommitted* (New York: Harcourt, Brace and World, 1965).

Klein, M. *The Psychoanalysis of Children* (London: The Hogarth Press, 1932).

Kobler, Arthur L., and Stotland, Ezra. *The End of Hope* (Glencoe, Ill.: The Free Press, 1964).

Kostrubala, Thaddeus, and McInerney, Marcia. "Suicide in Chicago: A Preliminary Statistical Attitudinal Survey," *Social Psychiatry*, 1966, *1* (3) 121-123.

Lester, David. "Suicide, Homicide, and the Effects of Socialization," *Journal of Personality and Social Psychology*, 1967, *5* (4) 466-468.

Levi, L. David, Fales, Catherine H., Stein, Marvin, and Sharp, Vernon H. "Separation and Attempted Suicide," *Archives of General Psychiatry*, 1966, *15* (2) 158-164.

Lewin, Kurt. *Dynamic Theory of Personality* (New York: McGraw-Hill, 1935).

Litman, Robert E. "Sigmund Freud on Suicide," *The Psychoanalytic Forum*, 1966, *1* (2) 205-221.

——— and Tabachnick, Norman. "Fatal One-Car Accidents," *Psychoanalytic Quarterly*, 1967, 36, 248-259.

Lorand, Sandor. "Adolescent Depression," *International Journal of Psychoanalysis*, 1967, 48, 53-60.

McClelland, David C. *The Achieving Society* (New York: The Free Press of Glencoe, 1967).

McCord, Joan, McCord, William, and Thurber, Emily. "Effects of Maternal Employment on Lower Class Boys," *Journal of Abnormal and Social Psychology*, 1963, 67, (2) 177-182.

Meaker, M. J. *Sudden Endings* (Garden City, N.Y.: Doubleday, 1964).

Meerloo, Joost A. M., *Suicide and Mass Suicide* (New York and London: Grune and Stratton, 1962).

Menninger, Karl A. *Man Against Himself* (New York: Harcourt, Brace, 1938).

Merton, Robert K. *Social Theory and Social Structure* (Glencoe, Ill.: The Free Press, 1949).

Miller, Daniel R., and Swanson, Guy E. *Inner Conflict and Defense* (New York: Holt, 1960).

National Office of Vital Statistics, *Vital Statistics*, Public Health Service, Washington, D. C. 1959.

Neuringer, Charles. "Methodological Problems in Suicide Research," *Journal of Consulting Psychiatry*, 1962, 26 (3) 273-278.

Otterland, Anders. *A Sociomedical Study of the Mortality in Merchant Seafarers* (London, William Heineman, Ltd., 1960).

Ødegård, Ø. "The Distribution of Mental Diseases in Norway," *Acta Psychiatrica et Neurologica Scandinavica*, 1945, *20*, 247 ff.

Østlyngen, Lisa Heber. "Har Barnepsykologisk Opplysningsarbeid Hatt Virkning?" *Norsk Pedagogisk Tidskrift*, 1960, *6*, 230-236.

Paerregaard, Grethe. *Selvmordforsøg og Selvmord i København* (Denmark: Aarhuus Stiftsbogtrykkerie, 1963).

Powell, Edwin H. "Occupation, Status, and Suicide," *American Sociological Review*, 1958, *20*, 55-59.

Provence, Sally, and Lipton, Rose C. *Infants in Institutions* (New York: International Universities Press, 1962).

Rado, S. "Hedonic Control, Action-Self, and the Depressive Spell," 1954. Revised 1955 *Collected Papers*, Vol. 1 (New York: Grune and Stratton, 1956).

——. "Psychodynamics of Depression from the Etiological Point of View," *Psychosomatic Medicine*, 1951, *13*.

Research and Statistics Division. *Vital Statistics*. Department of National Health and Welfare, Ottawa, Canada, 1960.

Rodnick, David. *The Norwegians* (Washington, D. C.: Public Affairs Press, 1955).

Rudfeld, Kirsten. *Selvmord i Danmark 1956: En Sociologisk Analyse Den Sociale Forskningsgruppe 1960*. Sociologisk Institut ved Københavns Universitet (mimeograph).

Sainsbury, Peter. *Suicide in London* (London: The Institute of Psychiatry, 1955).

Schiødt, E. "Traek af Danmarks Selvsmordstatistik," *Sociologiske Meddeleser* 7, Serie 1962.

Schrut, Albert. Suicidal Adolescents and Children," *Journal of the American Medical Association*, 1964 (13) 1103-1107.

Sears, R. R., Maccoby, E. E., and Levin, H. *Patterns of Child Rearing* (Evanston, Ill.: Row, Peterson, 1957).

——, Rau, Lucy, and Alpert, Richard. *Identification and Child Rearing* (Stanford, Calif.: Stanford University Press, 1965).

Shneidman, Edwin S. "Orientations toward Death: A Vital Aspect of the Study of Lives," *International Journal of Psychiatry*, 1966, 2 (2) 167-200.

——, and Farberow, Norman L., Eds. *Clues to Suicide* (New York: McGraw-Hill, 1957).

——. "A Socio-Psychological Investigation of Suicide," in David, Henry P., and Brenglemann, J. C., Eds. *Perspectives in Personality Research* (New York: Basic Books, 1960).

——. "The Los Angeles Suicide Prevention Center: A Demonstration of Public Health Facilities," *American Journal of Public Health*, 1965, 55, (1) 21-26.

Simonsen, Karen Margretha. *Examination of Children from Children's Homes and Day Nurseries* (Copenhagen: Nyt Nordisk Forlag Arnold Busck).

Spitz, R. A. "Hospitalism: An Inquiry into the Genesis of Psychiatric Conditions in Early Childhood," *The Psychoanalytic Study of the Child*, *1*, 53-74 (New York: International Universities Press, 1945).

——, and Wolf, K. M. "Anaclytic Depression: An Inquiry into the Genesis of Psychiatric Conditions in Early Childhood," *The Psychoanalytic Study of the Child*, 2, 313-342 (New York: International Universities Press, 1946).

Det Statistiske Departement. *Statistisk Årbog 1961*, Vol. 66, Copenhagen, Denmark, 1962.

Stengel, Erwin. "Some Unexplored Aspects of Suicide and Attempted Suicide," *Comprehensive Psychiatry*, 1960, *1*, 7-79.

——. *Suicide and Attempted Suicide* (Baltimore: Penguin Books, 1964).

—— and Cook, Nancy G. *Attempted Suicide: Its Social Significance and Effects*, Maudsley Monograph No. 4 (London: Chapman & Hall, 1958).

Straus, Jacqueline H., and Straus, Murray A. "Suicide, Homicide, and Social Structure in Ceylon," *American Journal of Sociology*, 1953, *58*, 461-469.

Svalastoga, Kaare. "The Family in Scandinavia," *Marriage and Family Living*, November, 1954, *16*, 374-380.

——— and Carlsson, Gosta. "Social Stratification and Social Mobility in Scandinavia," *Sociological Inquiry*, Winter, 1961.

Tabachnick, Norman. "Interpersonal Relations in Suicidal Attempts," *Archives in General Psychiatry*, 1961, *3*, 16-21.

Temoche, Abelardo, Puh, Thomas F., and MacMahon, Brian. "Suicide Rates Among Current and Former Mental Institution Patients," *The Journal of Nervous and Mental Diseases*, 1964, *138* (2) 124-130.

Verkho, V. *Homicides and Suicides in Finland and Their Dependence on National Character*. Scandinavian Studies in Sociology, 3 (Copenhagen: G.E.C. Gads Forlag, 1951).

Wechsberg, Joseph. "Letter from Berlin," *The New Yorker*, September 2, 1961.

Weiss, James M. A. "The Gamble with Death in Attempted Suicide," *Psychiatry*, 1957, *20*, 17-25.

West, D. J. *Murder Followed by Suicide* (Cambridge, Mass.: Harvard University Press, 1966).

White, Robert W. *Ego and Reality in Psychoanalytic Theory: A Proposal Regarding Independent Ego Energies* (New York: International Universities Press, 1963).

Wood, Arthur Lewis. "Crime and Aggression in Changing Ceylon." *Transactions of the American Philosophical Society*, New Series, Vol. 51, Part 8, 1961.

Index

THE LITERATURE OF DEATH AND DYING

Abrahamsson, Hans. **The Origin of Death:** Studies in African Mythology. 1951

Alden, Timothy. **A Collection of American Epitaphs and Inscriptions with Occasional Notes.** Five vols. in two. 1814

Austin, Mary. **Experiences Facing Death.** 1931

Bacon, Francis. **The Historie of Life and Death with Observations Naturall and Experimentall for the Prolongation of Life.** 1638

Barth, Karl. **The Resurrection of the Dead.** 1933

Bataille, Georges. **Death and Sensuality:** A Study of Eroticism and the Taboo. 1962

Bichat, [Marie François] Xavier. **Physiological Researches on Life and Death.** 1827

Browne, Thomas. **Hydriotaphia.** 1927

Carrington, Hereward. **Death:** Its Causes and Phenomena with Special Reference to Immortality. 1921

Comper, Frances M. M., editor. **The Book of the Craft of Dying and Other Early English Tracts Concerning Death.** 1917

Death and the Visual Arts. 1976

Death as a Speculative Theme in Religious, Scientific, and Social Thought. 1976

Donne, John. **Biathanatos.** 1930

Farber, Maurice L. **Theory of Suicide.** 1968

Fechner, Gustav Theodor. **The Little Book of Life After Death.** 1904

Frazer, James George. **The Fear of the Dead in Primitive Religion.** Three vols. in one. 1933/1934/1936

Fulton, Robert. **A Bibliography on Death, Grief and Bereavement:** 1845-1975. 1976

Gorer, Geoffrey. **Death, Grief, and Mourning.** 1965

Gruman, Gerald J. **A History of Ideas About the Prolongation of Life.** 1966

Henry, Andrew F. and James F. Short, Jr. **Suicide and Homicide.** 1954

Howells, W[illiam] D[ean], et al. **In After Days;** Thoughts on the Future Life. 1910

Irion, Paul E. **The Funeral:** Vestige or Value? 1966

Landsberg, Paul-Louis. **The Experience of Death:** The Moral Problem of Suicide. 1953

Maeterlinck, Maurice. **Before the Great Silence.** 1937

Maeterlinck, Maurice. **Death.** 1912

Metchnikoff, Élie. **The Nature of Man:** Studies in Optimistic Philosophy. 1910

Metchnikoff, Élie. **The Prolongation of Life:** Optimistic Studies. 1908

Munk, William. **Euthanasia.** 1887

Osler, William. **Science and Immortality.** 1904

Return to Life: Two Imaginings of the Lazarus Theme. 1976

Stephens, C[harles] A[sbury]. **Natural Salvation:** The Message of Science. 1905

Sulzberger, Cyrus. **My Brother Death.** 1961

Taylor, Jeremy. **The Rule and Exercises of Holy Dying.** 1819

Walker, G[eorge] A[lfred]. **Gatherings from Graveyards.** 1839

Warthin, Aldred Scott. **The Physician of the Dance of Death.** 1931

Whiter, Walter. **Dissertation on the Disorder of Death.** 1819

Whyte, Florence. **The Dance of Death in Spain and Catalonia.** 1931

Wolfenstein, Martha. **Disaster:** A Psychological Essay. 1957

Worcester, Alfred. **The Care of the Aged, the Dying, and the Dead.** 1950

Zandee, J[an]. **Death as an Enemy According to Ancient Egyptian Conceptions.** 1960